Mets
Triviology

Neil Shalin

TRIUMPH
BOOKS

Library of Congress Cataloging-in-Publication Data

Shalin, Neil, 1944–
 Mets triviology / Neil Shalin.
     p. cm.
 ISBN 978-1-60078-625-9
 1. New York Mets (Baseball team)—Miscellanea. I. Title.
 GV875.N45S48 2011
 796.357'64097471—dc23
                          2011035124

This book is available in quantity at special discounts for your group or organization. For further information, contact:

Triumph Books LLC
542 South Dearborn Street
Suite 750
Chicago, Illinois 60605
(312) 939-3330
Fax (312) 663-3557
www.triumphbooks.com

Printed in U.S.A.
ISBN: 978-1-60078-625-9
Design by Patricia Frey
Photos courtesy of AP Images unless otherwise noted

Contents

Introduction

Let's start right off with a trivia question.

Who was the first person to cross home plate safely at Shea Stadium in 1964, the Mets' first year playing there?

If you guessed Manny Mota or Bill Mazeroski of the Pirates, you'd be wrong. Ed Kranepool of the Mets is not correct either, nor is Joe Christopher.

The answer is yours truly, the author of this book.

I grew up in Flushing, near Queens College and the Long Island Expressway, about 2.5 miles from Shea Stadium.

It was a few nights before the Mets' scheduled April 17 home opener against the Pirates, and my friend Joel and I wanted to know how the new stadium was coming along. So we drove down there, turned off Roosevelt Avenue into the parking lot, and there were signs of activity from within.

We got out of Joel's car to see what was going on and whaddya know? The gate was open by the right-field bullpen, probably for construction vehicles to go in and out.

But we went in and walked across the field, expecting to be interrupted by a night watchman, or maybe one of those old movie matrons with the flashlight who terrorized our childhood.

But nobody stopped us. We saw several trucks in foul territory up the third-base line toward left field, and there were several pools of light in various places in the stands where construction workers were putting their finishing touches on seats or railings.

However, there was nobody to keep teenage boys from walking on the soon-to-be major league field.

Joel took his place on the mound and I went to the left-handed batters box, and we started playing shadow ball in the semidark of Shea Stadium. He was pitching for Pittsburgh and I, of course, was the Mets' batter.

I worked the count to 2-and-2, but Joel was getting impatient. He thought the game had gone far enough. Good, I had him rattled. I asked for one more pitch and it was a straight pretend fastball over the plate about waist high, right in my pretend wheelhouse.

I swung. Connected. I could tell by the sound of the ball hitting the bat that it would have distance. I began to run to first as I saw the backs of Virdon and Clemente furiously chasing it into the gap in deep right-center. I was halfway to second when the ball bounced near the warning track and took an odd carom high off the wall.

Of course, it being a new stadium, the usually steady-fielding Virdon didn't know the angles yet, and the ball took a high arc back over his head toward center, away from the charging Clemente.

As I rounded second I got it in my mind that *I'm going for it*. And at that moment I just knew that I was going all the way. As I came into third the coach was waving furiously for me to turn and head for home. I was so excited that I can't even tell you who the coach was. Nor do I remember the name of the next batter who was at home plate letting me know with a hand signal that I could make it standing up, which I did.

My teammates were congratulatory but low-key, as was I, because I had never been there before so I really didn't know how to act.

As I went into the dugout, I glanced back and saw Murtaugh at the mound taking the ball from Joel, and I noticed that Elroy Face was coming in from the bullpen.

Once in the dugout, there was nothing keeping me from following the open walkway back to the clubhouse. I went in. Joel soon followed. The fraternizing rules that forbade opponents from getting together were more lax in those days.

I can remember going in there and thinking that soon people like Willie Mays and Sandy Koufax will be sitting right here and getting ready to play a real major league game. Oops, I'd gone into the visitors' clubhouse. Later, when the game was over, I got an unmerciful ragging from the Pirates players. Pitcher Vern Law used language that wasn't fit for a deacon.

But I chalked it up to their disappointment that they suffered their first Shea Stadium loss to a mere journey-kid.

Now you know the answer to the first question about New York *Mets Triviology.*

After many years of riding a bus to the subway and then taking two or three trains to Yankee Stadium, the Polo Grounds, and Ebbets Field, we Queensites finally had a major league team.

True, it was only the Mets, to that point and for several years after the most spectacularly inept team baseball had ever seen. But that was okay. They would be better someday, and for the time being we had the chance to attend games right in the neighborhood, to see Willie and Roberto, Frank Robinson, Ernie Banks, Billy Williams, Bob Gibson, Bill White, Ken Boyer, Orlando Cepeda, and Brooklyn's own Tommy Davis, Joe Torre, and Sandy Koufax.

Looking back, everyone remembers how lovable the Mets were, but there's very little written about the fact that because they were so terrible, we got to see these immortals at their best, day after day, year after year.

And then came the Miracle Mets, and years later the '86 Mets, and while they've never built the Yankees-like dynasty we expected, it has been fun.

Shea Stadium is gone, but as of this writing, the faithful still have the likes of Jose Reyes, David Wright, and Johan Santana to keep their hopes alive.

In this book, we take you back in Mets history to remember the achievements—the good years and the bad—and all the fun that has been the past half century of Mets baseball. Choo-Choo, Hot Rod, and Marvelous Marv are all here, as are Tug, Doc, Cleon, and The Kid.

I hope you enjoy this book, that you learn something about Mets baseball through the years, and that you have fun testing your baseball knowledge.

Play ball.

A view of the 55,000-seat Shea Stadium as the Mets play their first game there on April 17, 1964.

One

First Base

The Rankings!
1. Keith Hernandez
2. Carlos Delgado
3. John Olerud
4. Ed Kranepool
5. Dave Magadan
6. John Milner
7. Eddie Murray
8. Dave Kingman
9. Donn Clendenon
10. Ike Davis

We've got a Hall of Famer in Eddie Murray in seventh place. Does that mean that the six guys ahead of him belong in the Hall of Fame?

While Hernandez, Delgado, and Olerud all have their Hall of Fame supporters, they rank at the top of the list because they contributed more to Mets winning teams and they played in New York longer than Murray, who was only a Met for two years.

Kranepool gets fourth place by virtue of the fact that he was a Met forever and made considerable contributions over the years. Magadan was a good spray hitter who started at first base and spent one year at third in the late '80s and early '90s.

Milner was a promising slugger when he came to the Mets but never developed the consistency that allowed him to make that next step.

Murray held down first base for two seasons toward the end of an illustrious career that was spent mostly with the Orioles. Kingman alternated between first base and the outfield, wherever it was thought he could do the least damage at any given time.

Clendenon was there only three seasons but was a key player on the 1969 Miracle Mets and the MVP of the World Series. And Davis, who should recover from his season-ending 2011 injury and go on to a long and fruitful career, enters the list at No. 10, with the potential to rise rapidly in the next few years. If he does, he'll be the first outstanding career first baseman, as everyone on this list but Kranepool had their best years with other teams.

Donn Clendenon

Maybe the '69 Miracle Mets weren't such a miracle after all.

We know they overtook the Cubs over the second half of the season before sweeping through the league championship series. Those were great achievements, and the Shea Stadium nine should be given its due.

And then, after losing the first game of the World Series to the "heavily favored Orioles," the Metsies swept the next four games.

It was a great victory, and it was an incredible improvement for one team to make after finishing ninth the year before. In fact, in their first seven years of existence, the Mets *never* finished higher than ninth.

But a combination of extraordinary circumstances turned the Mets into a damned-good team that year, and they were just better than everyone else. There's nothing miraculous about that.

First, they had good pitching. Most of the hurlers—namely Tom Seaver, Jerry Koosman, Gary Gentry, Tug McGraw, and Nolan Ryan—were young and ready to enter the prime of their careers.

If a team has to be strong up the middle, the Mets certainly were. They had a savvy veteran catcher in Jerry Grote and a sharp-fielding shortstop in Bud Harrelson. Add Tommie Agee in center field and few teams could match their central defense.

Agee and his old friend, Mets veteran Cleon Jones, both had great years, so the outfield did have some pop.

While there may not have been outstanding players at the other positions, they were talented enough to rise to the opportunity presented by manager Gil Hodges' lefty-righty platoon system at first base, second base, third base, and right field.

And, as it turned out there was enough depth around the field, in the rotation, and in the bullpen to give the manager flexibility and the fans a different hero every day in the chase for the pennant.

And then there was the addition of the missing ingredient. That little bit of spice that made the recipe work. On June 15, the Mets traded for an established big-league slugger in a three-way trade with the Astros and Expos.

For years, Donn Clendenon had been the starting first baseman in a powerful Pittsburgh lineup that included Roberto Clemente and Willie Stargell. He was expendable because of some young talent coming out of the Pittsburgh farm system. He was sent to the Expos but only lasted there a few months until he was sent on to the Mets.

Clendenon, who averaged about 23 homers and 80 RBIs a season in Pittsburgh, was platooned with Ed Kranepool at first base. He hit 12 home runs and knocked in 37 runs during that amazing drive to overtake the Cubs.

He gave the Mets a big bat in the middle of the lineup, and he helped give them attitude.

"He was the catalyst on our team," said outfielder Art Shamsky to author Stanley Cohen for his book, *A Magic Season.* "You can talk about our pitching, which was great, and whatever else, but until June [we] were just a potentially good team."

In that first year of division play, the Mets were nine games behind the Cubs in the NL East when Clendenon joined the team.

After a slow start, the new first baseman got hot at the end of August. He hit a 10th-inning home run to give the Mets a 3–2 win over the Giants, helping the team pull to within 2½ games of the division leader by the time the Cubs came to Flushing for a two-game series on September 8.

The New Yorkers swept the series to pull within a half game, with Clendenon hitting a two-run homer in the second game.

The Mets increased their winning streak to 10 in a row, which put them 3½ games ahead of the Cubs. Then, on September 24, Clendenon hit a pair of homers in a game against the Cardinals, and the team clinched the NL East.

The Mets won 39 of their last 50 games and ended the season with a 100–62 record, eight games ahead of the Cubs.

Clendenon was not used in the three-game sweep in the first-ever NLCS, but he did play in the World Series, which became the lasting memory of his career.

The Mets lost the first game 4–1 but played well enough to prove to themselves that they could compete with the Orioles.

"I swear, we came into the clubhouse more confident than we had left it," said Tom Seaver years later. "Somebody—I think it was Clendenon—yelled out, 'Dammit, we can beat these guys!' And we believed it...The feeling wasn't that we had lost, but, 'Hey, we nearly won that game!' We hadn't been more than a hit or two from turning it around. It hit us like a ton of bricks."

Clendenon had two hits in that first game, scoring the team's only run in the 4–1 loss.

And then he came back to hit early solo shots in Games 2 and 4 to give the Mets a 1–0 lead in each game.

The Mets had the favored Orioles of Frank Robinson, Brooks Robinson, and Jim Palmer on the ropes.

But the O's jumped out to a 3–0 lead in Game 5.

Cleon Jones led off the sixth and was hit by a Dave McNally pitch, but umpire Lou DiMuro said the pitch missed him. Mets manager Gil Hodges argued the call, and when he showed the ump a shoe polish smudge on the ball, DiMuro reversed his call and signaled Jones to take his base.

Clendenon came to the plate and hit a two-run blast to make the score 3–2, and the Mets went on to win 5–2 to complete the "Miracle."

Clendenon finished the series with three home runs and four RBIs, batting .357 to win the Series MVP award. His three home runs set a record for home runs in a five-game series.

"You could count on the big man. We all knew that," outfielder Ron Swoboda said, reflecting on that championship season.

"Clendenon was probably the key to our whole season," Shamsky said. "Because when he came over we really came alive."

In 1970, Clendenon, then 34, had one more big season, giving the Mets 22 home runs, 97 RBIs, and a .288 average, but it is his contribution to the Miracle that is his lasting legacy.

Carlos Delgado

Mets fans caught the tail end of the best of Carlos Delgado, just before age and injuries eroded his once-brilliant skills. When he finally retired after the 2009 season, Delgado had produced 473 home runs and 1,512 RBIs, with a .383 OBP and a .546 slugging percentage over a 17-year career, mostly with the Blue Jays.

But Delgado, who joined the Mets in '06 at the age of 34, was the cleanup hitter in an extraordinary lineup that also included Jose Reyes, Carlos Beltran, and David Wright. The Mets won 96 games that year, tying them with the Yankees for the best record in baseball. They lost to the Cardinals in seven games in the NLCS.

In '07, he got off to a slow start but still finished with 24 round-trippers and 87 RBIs. He bounced back the following year with 38 homers and 115 ribbies in a season that included a 5-for-5 day with a walk-off RBI against the Cardinals. It also included a game against the Braves in which he hit a pair of three-run homers.

Delgado's last year was almost a total loss due to a hip injury that would force him to retire before the '10 season.

"He was unbelievable for us when he was healthy," said Reyes to the *New York Daily News*. "And he taught me how to play the right way."

When Delgado retired, former Toronto teammate Vernon Wells lamented that the first basemen fell short of reaching the 500–home run mark and called him one of the great power hitters of his generation.

"He had some of the most impressive pop that you'll see in a ballplayer—to all fields. And when he hit the ball, it wasn't coming down," Wells said.

"The ball explodes off his bat," said Roger Clemens. "It sounds louder off his bat than anybody else's."

Besides his impressive record on the diamond, Delgado is one of those rare players who was admired for his character. Many of his teammates lauded Delgado for his strong personality and the influence he had on their lives.

"Carlos is a great leader—a leader by example and every other way," said former teammate David Wells.

"What separates him from the other superstars is that he doesn't have the big ego," said former teammate Shawn Green. "Baseball really isn't his life. If he had to quit tomorrow, I know he'd find something else as challenging, and he'd be a big success at it."

Former Mets manager Willie Randolph said of Delgado, "He's a man of his word, he's a man of conviction, and he's not afraid to speak his mind. I respect him for that."

Throughout his public life, Delgado has been a passionate supporter of his native Puerto Rico. He's also been open about his political views, which include a consistent stand as a peace activist. He was opposed to the U.S. using the island of Vieques, Puerto Rico, as a bombing target-practice facility, and he was against the invasion and occupation of Iraq.

"It's a very terrible thing that happened on September 11," said Delgado to the *Toronto Star*. "It's also a terrible thing that happened in Afghanistan and Iran.... I just feel so sad for the families that lost relatives and loved ones in the war. But I think it's the stupidest war ever."

In '04, at Yankee Stadium, he was booed for not standing for the playing of "God Bless America," which he said came to be equated with a war he didn't believe in.

Like his hero Robert Clemente, Delgado was not only open about his beliefs, but he was active in numerous charities and was proud to represent Puerto Rico in the majors.

"As for his charity work, Delgado often visited hospitals in his hometown, bringing toys to hospitalized children. He formed the nonprofit organization Extra Bases, Inc. to assist Puerto Rican youth, donated video-conference equipment to allow a Puerto Rican hospital to link with a Boston hospital for remote diagnosis through telemedicine, and he's been a generous contributor to the Puerto Rican public education system.

In '06, Delgado was awarded the Roberto Clemente Award, which goes to the player who best exemplifies humanitarianism and sportsmanship.

"Carlos has the same stature as Roberto Clemente," said former major leaguer Cookie Rojas. "Roberto always tried to help the Latin players and people and wanted to leave something behind. He wanted to make people better. Carlos has all the same dignity and the same pride."

Perhaps former Blue Jays manager Cito Gaston said it best: "If you had a son, you'd like him to be like Carlos."

1. Dave Kingman led the NL in homers as a New York Met in 1982, with 37, but he led all of baseball in 1979, with a career-high 48. What team was he playing for at the time?

2. Donn Clendenon was the Pirates' first baseman through most of the 1960s. Name three of his teammates—all of whom are position players and starters—who are in the Hall of Fame.

3. Ed Kranepool graduated from James Monroe High School in the Bronx. Which Hall of Fame first baseman was also a Monroe graduate?

4. In 1993, John Olerud won the AL batting crown, hitting .363 as a member of the Toronto Blue Jays. Who finished second?

5. Who was the National League batting champion in 1993?

6. Keith Hernandez batted .344 to win the NL batting title in 1979 as a member of the St. Louis Cardinals. Who finished second?

7. Who was the AL batting champion in 1979?

8. Which one of these players never played first base for the Mets?
   a. Rico Brogna
   b. Mo Vaughn
   c. Butch Huskey
   d. Ferris Fain

9. Who was the starting first baseman for the Mets on Opening Day in their inaugural year, 1962?

10. Keith Hernandez was the Mets' Opening Day first baseman every year between 1984 and 1989. Who was the team's Opening Day starter in 1990?

Answers

1. Chicago Cubs
2. Roberto Clemente, Bill Mazeroski, and Willie Stargell
3. Hank Greenberg
4. Paul Molitor (.332)
5. Andres Galarraga (.370)
6. Pete Rose (.331)
7. Fred Lynn (.333)
8. d. Ferris Fain
9. Gil Hodges
10. Mike Marshall

Two

Second Base

The Rankings!
1. Felix Millan
2. Wally Backman
3. Jeff Kent
4. Ron Hunt
5. Greg Jefferies
6. Ken Boswell
7. Doug Flynn
8. Carlos Baerga
9. Tim Teufel
10. Roberto Alomar

The New York Mets need a second baseman. They've always needed a second baseman. Our top 10 has some pretty good ballplayers, but none who were able to grab the job and hold on to it for a decade.

Millan had a nice career with the Braves, and then spent five years with the Mets. Backman was a tough little scrapper who served the team well in the years surrounding the '86 championship, but he often platooned with Teufel.

Kent was a slugger who was traded away before he really blossomed into a power hitter elsewhere, and Hunt was the team's first homegrown star, but he spent most of his career on other NL teams.

Jefferies was a great prospect as a Met but never really found a position. Still, he was good, although not as good as he was touted to be.

Boswell, the starting second baseman on the '69 team, was never really a full-timer in his eight seasons with the club. Flynn was a steady fielder who held the job for a number of years on bad teams, but his offense was a liability. Baerga saw better days with other clubs, and Alomar certainly did not look like a Hall of Famer when he played for the Mets.

We're still looking for our first star second sacker.

Ron Hunt

Hunt holds a particularly warm place in the hearts of old Mets fans because he was really the first young star they had to root for.

He was a scrappy 22-year-old when he came up in 1963, and he finished second in the Rookie of the Year voting that year to Pete Rose. Charlie Hustle was a second baseman with the Growing Red Machine during his first three years, before he was moved to other positions to make room for Joe Morgan, who was acquired in a trade from Houston.

Rose hit .273 and scored 101 runs that year, while Hunt hit .272 with 10 homers and 42 RBIs. They had an identical .334 OBP, and neither was noted for his range in the field.

The following year was key to the argument that has raged over succeeding generations. Who was better: Rose or Hunt?

In '64, Hunt was voted to the NL All-Star Game, which was held at brand-new Shea Stadium in Queens. He finished the year with a .303 average to Rose's .269. All of Metdom was convinced at this point that it had the better of the two promising second sackers.

The Mets infielder, in his attempt to get on base any way he could, also started to show a penchant for *getting* hit. In his first year he took 13 for the team, followed by 16 in his second season.

The Flushing Faithful stopped paying attention to the Hunt vs. Rose debate after that. They had seen enough.

Hunt had some injury problems in '65 and would play only one more year in New York before moving on to the Dodgers for a season, the Giants for three, and the Expos for four before finishing up with the Cardinals.

By the time he reached San Francisco he had improved the HBP to an art form, leading the league in plunks seven straight years with a league record of 50 as a 1971 Expo. He played the most games of his career that year, 152, and had his highest OBP at .402.

He also struck out fewer times (41) than he was hit, and that happened again two years later when he hit a career-high .309.

During that season, Hunt was hit by pitcher Bill Bonham three of the four times he faced him. Hunt had six games in which he was hit by a pitch at least twice.

Hunt told *Baseball Digest's* Al Doyle that he practiced his getting-hit stance in front of a mirror in full uniform to make sure he was perfect.

"I'd stand right on top of the plate," he said. "An inside pitch had to be right on the corner or it would hit me. The umpire never called me for getting hit on purpose."

When he was with the Giants, Hunt was told by Willie McCovey, "If you're crazy enough to go after that record you can have it."

Hunt reported that he never had any broken bones, but he played with a lot of "bruises and ouches."

He finished his career with a .273 lifetime batting average and a .368 OBP. He was hit by 243 pitches.

And what happened to this Rose fellow?

In 24 seasons he hit .305, made 17 All-Star appearances, punched out an all-time record 4,256 hits, scored 2,165 runs, and had 166 home runs and 1,314 RBIs.

Now from a Mets fan's perspective, Hunt gets the advantage for having remained a second baseman throughout his career, while they couldn't find a steady position for Rose, who bounced around playing third, first, and all three outfield positions over the years.

And it was Hunt who once said, "Some people give their bodies to science; I give mine to baseball."

And while Hunt was proving himself as the most courageous player in the game, what was Rose doing? All he did was earn the nickname "Charlie Hustle."

And how important is that? Bob Meusel, the Yankees outfielder in the '20s, had this to say about the value of hustling.

"Hustling is rather overrated in baseball," Meusel told *Baseball Magazine* in 1926. "It's a showy quality that looks well and counts for little."

So you make the call. Who was better: Ron Hunt or Pete Rose? It's just a travesty that Ron Hunt hasn't made the Hall of Fame. Just ask any old, rabid Mets fan.

And speaking of those early Mets fans and the love they felt for the ballplayers on their miserable teams in the early and mid-'60s, there was a special place in their hearts for utility man Rod Kanehl.

Rod Kanehl

Hot Rod joined the Mets after eight years in the Yankees farm system, and he made the team because manager Casey Stengel liked his aggressive style. Casey remembered Kanehl leaping over the fence to catch a ball during a Yankees exhibition game years before.

The manager had to fight his boss George Weiss to keep Kanehl on the roster, and Hot Rod remained a Met for three seasons, playing every position but pitcher and catcher.

"I remembered him," Stengel said. "He climbed a fence for me once."

The New York fans got their first view of Kanehl in a televised exhibition game from Florida when, as a pinch-hitter, he hit a check-swing, two-run double off Dodger ace Sandy Koufax to tie a game that the Mets eventually won. Mets fans were ready to embrace the former Yankees farmhand by the time the team got to New York to start the season.

And that year, through all that futility, the hustling Kanehl gave the team some thrills.

On April 28, 1962, Kanehl slid home with the winning run against the Phillies. He scored from second on a wild pitch to give the Mets the first home victory in their history after seven losses.

He went on to score the winning run in nine of the Mets' first 12 victories. The 11th and 12th wins came as both ends of a doubleheader in late May against the Braves. Craig Anderson was the winning pitcher in both games. In July, Kanehl hit the Mets' first grand slam in a game against the Cardinals at the Polo Grounds.

The consummate utility man, in '62 Kanehl was the first Met to play every position but pitcher and catcher. He didn't play any position really well, but boy did he hustle, and boy did the fans respond to his style and personality.

Kanehl later claimed that the first banner fans displayed at the Polo Grounds said, "We love the Mets," and written under it was, "and Rod Kanehl."

Hot Rod also got the last pinch-hit at the Polo Grounds before it was torn down, following the '64 season.

Everyone knew that Kanehl was Casey's favorite player because if it wasn't for the Old Perfessor, the utility man may never have made it to the majors.

Kanehl's major league career lasted only three years, and he played a total of 133 games, mostly at second and third base. He hit .248 and had four home runs and eight stolen bases.

After the '64 season, he was sent to the minors. When his career ended, Kanehl repeatedly tried to stay in the game, but he was never able to secure a position in baseball.

"I thought there would always be room for a guy who knows the game and has some intelligence," a disappointed Kanehl told *Sports Illustrated*. "I know the game from underneath. I know what goes on in the mind of a mediocre ballplayer. I know what it's like to be a bad hitter. I know what it's like to have to battle every time you come up to the plate."

In his later years he worked in construction, sold insurance, and owned a restaurant.

When Casey Stengel died in 1975, Kanehl was the only former Met who went to his funeral in Glendale, California.

Looking back on his career, Kanehl, who died in 2004 at the age of 70, said, "Baseball is a lot like life. The line drives are caught, the squibbles go for base hits. It's an unfair game."

He may not have been one of the greatest major leaguers, but it *is* fair that Rod Kanehl left his mark. He was the Mets' first legitimate hero.

Quiz!

1. Who was the Mets' starting second baseman in their inaugural year, 1962?
2. Name the two Mets who played second base in the 1969 World Series.
3. Who was the Mets' second baseman in the 1973 World Series?
4. Name the two Mets who played second base in the 1986 World Series.
5. Who was the Mets' second baseman in the 2000 World Series?
6. Which Mets second baseman has been inducted into the Baseball Hall of Fame?
7. Which Mets second baseman has career totals of 377 home runs and 1,518 RBIs?
8. Who led the NL in doubles in 1990, with 40?
9. Who finished his 18-year big league career with the Mets and then went on to manage the team?
10. Which Mets manager won three Gold Gloves as a second baseman with the Orioles?

Answers

1. Charlie Neal
2. Ken Boswell and Al Weis
3. Felix Millan
4. Wally Backman and Tim Teufel
5. Edgardo Alfonzo
6. Roberto Alomar
7. Jeff Kent
8. Gregg Jefferies
9. Willie Randolph
10. Davey Johnson

Three

Shortstop

The Rankings!
1. Jose Reyes
2. Bud Harrelson
3. Rey Ordonez
4. Rafael Santana
5. Roy McMillan
6. Jose Vizcaino
7. Frank Taveras
8. Kevin Elster
9. Ron Gardenhire
10. Tim Foli

The best shortstop in Mets history is playing right now. All Reyes has to do is stay healthy and stay consistent, and he could be remembered as one of the best shortstops of his time.

Harrelson, while never a great hitter, made the defense solid and was a team leader on the Mets' first successful clubs. He and

Reyes successfully swipes second yet again.

Cleon Jones were the first two nonpitching prospects who actually delivered and played a big part in the team's early success.

In his prime, Ordonez was regarded as the best fielder in the league, while anchoring a great infield foursome that also included John Olerud, Edgardo Alfonzo, and Robin Ventura.

After that, the list is all good-field, no-hit defenders, journeymen, and okay guys, except McMillan, who was considered the top defensive shortstop in the league for a decade before he came to the Mets, by which time he had become just another okay, good-field, no-hit journeyman.

In conclusion, after Reyes and Harrelson, there's not too much to get excited about here.

Jose Reyes

By the time you read this, Jose Reyes, who along with David Wright has been the face of the Mets franchise since 2004, could be wearing another team's uniform.

The combination of the Mets' financial woes and the contract that Reyes will be seeking after the 2011 season may force the New Yorkers to trade their All-Star shortstop, or let him go via free agency, much to the unhappiness of the team's fans.

Despite rumors of secret negotiations that are designed to keep Reyes at the club, Jose is saying he won't discuss a new contract until after the season, when he will be a free agent.

"Right now, I don't want any distractions," Reyes told Adam Rubin of ESPN New York. "I just want to continue to play. We're going to have plenty of time in the off-season to make this happen."

But Jose is careful to point out that this in no way should be interpreted as an indication of whether he'll sign with the only team he's ever known, or if he'll test the market that promises a major payday for the superstar.

"Nothing changed," Reyes said. "I want to stay here. Like I've always said, I want to be a New York Met all my career."

Reyes and Wright have been the cornerstones of the franchise for years. Mets fans have a love affair with both players and hope for the day when the team will build around them in order to compete for the pennant again.

The Dominican shortstop, who plays the game with infectious exuberance and joy, has grown in recent years as a hitter, in the field, and as one of baseball's great threats on the base paths.

He's a four-time All-Star, he's led the AL in stolen bases three times, and all of baseball in triples three times. He was also the league leader in hits in '08. Not to mention, he's got great range in the field.

At the age of 28, Reyes is already the team's all-time leader in both triples and stolen bases. He has a .292 career batting average, some pop in his bat, and in recent years he's become a more patient hitter.

Yankees third baseman Alex Rodriguez said that he believes Reyes is now the best player in the game.

"They have the world's greatest player playing shortstop over there, and the most exciting," Rodriguez said. "I turn on the TV every time I get a chance to watch him."

He's good to score about 100 runs a year when he's been healthy. Health could be the one factor that makes other teams reluctant to pay top dollar for Reyes in the free agent market.

He has been injured frequently, starting in his rookie year ('03) when he spent time on the disabled list with a sprained ankle. The following year he missed most of the first half of the season with a strained hamstring. But he showed his superstar potential when he remained basically healthy the next four years, turning in seasons that won him votes in the MVP balloting.

Then in May '09, he aggravated a calf injury that put him on the disabled list for the rest of the season and required off-season surgery.

In 2010, Reyes landed on the DL again in April with a hyperactive thyroid. He also missed significant time at various points in the season with an oblique injury.

Mets owner Fred Wilpon, who is involved in a lawsuit stemming from ownership's dealings with Bernie Madoff, thinks that the injuries will keep the shortstop from getting the maximum payoff commensurate with his skills.

"He thinks he's going to get Carl Crawford money," Wilpon told the *New Yorker*. "He's had everything wrong with him. He won't get it."

Roy McMillan

Back in the 1960s, the Mets had another shortstop who caused baseball people to reach back into their bag of superlatives. But, sadly, by the time Roy McMillan came to the Mets he had lost a step from his 10-year stint with the Reds and then another three years during which he was generally regarded as the best-fielding shortstop in the game.

"Many who saw McMillan play suggested that he might be the greatest shortstop ever," said Bill James to the *Sporting News*. "He had tremendous range; going left, right, and everywhere to turn base hits into double plays."

McMillan was the Gold Glove winner at shortstop for 1957, '58, and '59, the first three years of the award.

The skinny Texan also played three years with the Braves before coming to the Mets, where he finished his 16-season career in '66.

Hall of Famer Pie Traynor was one of many who was impressed by McMillan's defense. "McMillan makes his own bounces. He's the only present-day shortstop who can do that...he can take the ball on the half hop all the time, a very tough play," Traynor said.

McMillan had a lifetime batting average of .243, but he could knock in a run when needed, and he hit the occasional home run, finishing his career with 68 home runs and 594 RBIs.

When McMillan came up to the Reds in '51 they were a second-division ballclub. However, by the time the mid-'50s came around, the team was a contender, though usually behind the Dodgers and the Braves.

They were led by the smooth double-play combination of McMillan and Johnny Temple and a lineup of big bats that included Hall of Famer Frank Robinson, Ted Kluszewski, and Gus Bell. In fact, the '56 Reds, led by NL Rookie of the Year Robinson, tied the single-season home run record with 221. McMillan, who played in the All-Star Game in both '56 and '57, contributed only three, but he did drive in a career-high 62 runs. Local writers named him the team's most valuable player, and he finished sixth in the league MVP voting.

Leo Durocher, a former major league shortstop, called McMillan "the best defensive shortstop in the game today."

Announcers called him "Mr. Shortstop" and "the Suction Cup." He was durable, too. McMillan played in 150 games or more eight times, including 157 with the Mets in '57.

One of the highlights of his Mets career was against the Giants in that marathon 23-inning game in '64. McMillan started a triple play in that game.

Bud Harrelson

If Mets fans didn't have reason enough to root against Pete Rose before, they certainly did after Game 3 of the 1973 playoffs between the Mets and the Reds.

It was at Shea Stadium. The Mets were winning 9–2 in the top of the ninth, with the Reds coming up to bat.

Rose singled with one out. Then Joe Morgan followed with a ground ball wide of first. John Milner picked it up and fired to shortstop Bud Harrelson covering second. Harrelson threw it back to Milner to complete the double play.

Rose slid into second with his hands high and elbowed the 140-pound Harrelson. The Mets shortstop then went after the 200-pound Rose and the two went to the ground fighting.

"He came after me after I threw the ball," Harrelson said. "I didn't like what he did. I just wanted to tell him I'm not a punching bag. I thought he got me late."

Rose claimed it was the way he always slid. "He called me a name and I grabbed him. He started coming at me and we went down. I play hard. I don't play dirty. I could have leveled him."

Rose refused to apologize because he thought he did the right thing. "I might slide harder tomorrow," Rose said.

The next inning, when Rose went out to left field to play his position, he got the full razzing from the crowd. Someone even threw a whisky bottle at him. That caused manager Sparky Anderson to pull the team from the field and into the clubhouse.

The crowd continued to be loud and unruly.

NL President Chub Feeney went out to huddle with the umpires, and they decided to send a contingent of Mets out to left field to try to calm the crowd.

Manager Yogi Berra went, along with Willie Mays, Tom Seaver, Cleon Jones, and Rusty Staub.

Yogi told the crowd to be quiet, reminding them that if play couldn't be resumed the Reds would win in a forfeit, which would be ridiculous since the Mets were winning 9–2. The crowd got quiet.

Rose later claimed that the hard slide was payback for a pitch that Mets pitcher Jerry Koosman had thrown too close to him when he was up at bat.

The Mets won the game. The Reds took Game 4 2–1 in 12 innings, and then the Mets won Game 5 by a score of 7–2 to win the series.

New York then moved on to the World Series, where they lost four games to three to the AL champion A's in the second of their three straight World Series victories.

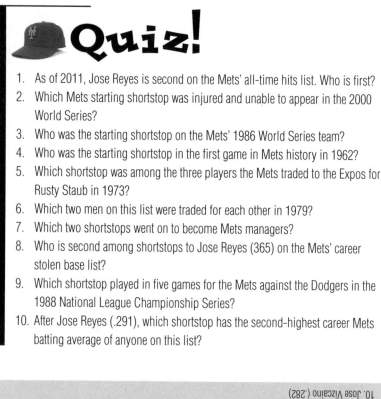

Quiz!

1. As of 2011, Jose Reyes is second on the Mets' all-time hits list. Who is first?
2. Which Mets starting shortstop was injured and unable to appear in the 2000 World Series?
3. Who was the starting shortstop on the Mets' 1986 World Series team?
4. Who was the starting shortstop in the first game in Mets history in 1962?
5. Which shortstop was among the three players the Mets traded to the Expos for Rusty Staub in 1973?
6. Which two men on this list were traded for each other in 1979?
7. Which two shortstops went on to become Mets managers?
8. Who is second among shortstops to Jose Reyes (365) on the Mets' career stolen base list?
9. Which shortstop played in five games for the Mets against the Dodgers in the 1988 National League Championship Series?
10. After Jose Reyes (.291), which shortstop has the second-highest career Mets batting average of anyone on this list?

Answers

1. Ed Kranepool (1,418 hits)
2. Rey Ordonez
3. Rafael Santana
4. Felix Mantilla
5. Tim Foli
6. The Mets traded Foli to the Pirates for Frank Taveras.
7. Bud Harrelson and Roy McMillian
8. Bud Harrelson (115) is the next shortstop in stolen bases. He's eighth overall among all Mets.
9. Kevin Elster
10. Jose Vizcaino (.282)

Four

Third Base

The Rankings!
1. David Wright
2. Edgardo Alfonzo
3. Howard Johnson
4. Robin Ventura
5. Hubie Brooks
6. Wayne Garrett
7. Ray Knight
8. Ed Charles
9. Charley Smith
10. Ken Boyer

David Wright, if he continues his so-far brilliant career with the Mets, could turn out to be the best position player the Mets ever had. The same could be said for Jose Reyes. Since 2004, the two have been the heart of a team that has promised so much and delivered so little, due to a combination of injury-riddled seasons and just poor baseball down the stretch.

However, if Wright and Reyes stick around, stay healthy, and keep producing, and if the Mets add the talent around them to lead to some postseason glory, both infielders could be headed to the Hall of Fame.

Wright, though only 28, already takes his place at the head of the Mets third-base list. Alfonzo, who also played extensively at second base, is ranked just ahead of HoJo in second place. Robin Ventura, one of the premier third sackers of the day for a decade with the White Sox, also gave the Mets a few stellar seasons.

The others are short-term solutions to the position who were cultivated in the Mets' farm system, such as Brooks and Garrett; or those brought over from other teams who made specific contributions to winning seasons (Knight and Charles), disappointments (Smith), and a former great who served the Mets briefly (Boyer).

But, the top three are the historical strength of the position, Mets who served the team with distinction for an extended period of time.

David Wright

Until a concussion from a beaning that forced him to miss a chunk of 2009 and a 2011 back injury that also put him on the shelf for a long spell, Wright was—and hopefully will be again—the kind of position player a team dreams about.

Pencil him into your lineup for 150 games when he's 21 years old and then forget about the position for 16 or 17 years while he piles up Hall of Fame numbers.

We just have to hope that his recent serious injuries don't sidetrack his march to Cooperstown, just as the sure-shot Hall of Fame careers of third basemen such as Al Rosen and recently Scott Rolen and Eric Chavez were derailed because of a run of physical ailments.

If Wright or Reyes is traded by the time you read this, it means that the Mets are starting from scratch to build a contending team. Whatever else has been wrong with the team the past few years, the left side of the infield is set, and these two players are in their prime years.

And it's obvious that if Wright has anything to say about it, he's in New York for the long haul. "I love being a Met," Wright has said. "It was my favorite team growing up, so to be a Met to me is very special."

From the day the Norfolk, Virginia, native started a game against the Expos in July of '04, Wright has been the team's starting third baseman. He made a great first impression on the (then) Shea Stadium faithful by delivering 14 home runs and 40 RBIs with a .293 average in his first half-season.

The following year, Wright's first full season in the majors, he batted .306 (.388 OBP), with 27 homers and 102 RBIs, his first of five 25-plus homer seasons and 100-plus RBIs to date.

He had to wait until '06 to make his first of five straight All-Star appearances, and in '07 and '08 he won both the Silver Slugger and the Gold Glove.

Now in his eighth season (2011), he has a lifetime average of .302. He's averaged 27 homers and 106 RBIs a year, and he's good for 80 walks per season,. He also averages 23 stolen bases per year.

Former teammate and future Hall of Famer Mike Piazza noticed early on that Wright was something special. "He's got a great approach at the plate, a lot of tools, and he's continuing to learn," Piazza said.

"I'm always looking to improve," said Wright. "And every year I want to do better than the year before."

And Wright has impressed all observers with his consistency and his mature demeanor both on and off the field. He is generally

Wright puts another one in the seats at Shea in a 2006 game against the Reds.

considered one of the most polite and humble ballplayers in the majors.

"I'm very confident in what I do, but I'd like to think I don't ever show any kind of cockiness or overconfidence," Wright said.

He has been involved in numerous programs for charity, is accommodating with fans and the press, and has been the face of the team on local and national TV shows.

David Wright is a complete ballplayer and a fine citizen, and that combination has not been common in Mets history.

Early on, former Met Joe McEwing said of Wright, "It's definitely refreshing the way he handles himself and the way he goes about his business. He's a special player and a special person."

Edgardo Alfonzo

There is another former Met who has attained that status of complete ballplayer and fine citizen and that's infielder Edgardo Alfonzo, perhaps the most underrated player in the team's 50-year history.

We've got Fonzie rated as the No. 2 Mets third baseman of all time, although he did spend a lot of time as a second baseman.

Throughout his career, Alfonzo proved to be the consummate team guy, moving between the two positions several times to help the Mets when they acquired Carlos Baerga to play second in 1997, then Robins Venture to play third in '99, and finally when Hall of Famer Roberto Alomar became the team's second baseman in 2002.

Between '97 and '04 (the last two years with the Giants), he averaged .291 (.371 OPS), 17 home runs, and 77 RBIs.

But in '99 and '00, when the Mets went to the postseason, Fonzie had his two biggest years at the plate. This while part of the Mets' "best infield of all time" that also included John Olerud at first base, light-hitting Rey Ordonez at shortstop, and Ventura at third.

Ventura talked about Alfonzo with T.J. Quinn in the *New York Daily News*, saying, "He's by far the best player on the team. I thought I knew how good he was, but you have to see him every day. He doesn't do anything wrong."

Outfielder Jay Payton said about Alfonzo, "He's my MVP. The guy's just amazing. I don't even know how to describe it."

Though he gained fame as a clutch performer, coming up with key hits and big plays in the field numerous times in his Mets career, it was on August 30, 1999, in a game against the Astros, that Fonzie authored one of the all-time great days at the plate in Mets history.

Hitting in the second slot and playing second base, Alfonzo slugged a solo home run in the top of the first. The Mets jumped out to a 7–0 lead with a six-run rally in the second inning that included Alfonzo's single to right. He later scored on an Olerud double. His third time up was in the fourth inning, and he smashed his second home run of the game to make it 9–0. Then he led off the sixth with his third homer of the game.

(For those of you keeping score at home, he was 4-for-4 at that point.)

Fonzie led off the eighth with a single to left and scored his fifth run of the game. In the ninth he lined to right for an RBI double and later scored the Mets' 17th and final run. They won 17–1.

He finished the day with six hits in six at-bats, three home runs, six runs scored, and five RBIs.

It was also memorable because his performance set single-game team records for hits, runs, and total bases (16), as well as tying the record for home runs. He was one of only seven Mets in history to hit three home runs in one game.

Though he wasn't flashy, and he probably didn't get enough credit from the general public, Alfonzo was recognized as one of the league's better players by baseball insiders.

Former Mets general manager Omar Minaya told T.J. Quinn of the *Daily News* that Alfonzo played the old style of baseball. "He isn't flashy and he isn't built like some of the classic sluggers. He does all the little things in the game. That's the way they play in Venezuela. They expect you to bunt, they expect you to get the guy over—the little things."

Throughout his career, Alfonzo, like Wright, was a shining example of how to play the game with excellence and grace and how to conduct himself as a professional, both on and off the field.

"I try to help. I try to play my part in the game," he said. Alfonzo is trying to do the little things right in life as well. "I just try to be a good role model for my kids and for the kids of the world, especially in the Latin countries."

Alfonzo ranks in the top 10 in most offensive categories for the Mets. He's fifth in career hits, runs, and doubles; sixth in batting average; seventh in walks and OBP; eighth in games played; and ninth in home runs and at-bats.

Mets Who Have Hit Three Home Runs in One Game:

Jose Reyes	at Philadelphia	August 15, 2006
Edgardo Alfonzo	at Houston	August 30, 1999
Gary Carter	at San Diego	September 3, 1985
Darryl Strawberry	at Chicago	August 5, 1985
Claudell Washington	at Los Angeles	June 22, 1980
Dave Kingman	at Los Angeles	June 4, 1976
Jim Hickman	at St. Louis	September 3, 1965

 **Quiz!**

1. David Wright has already risen to second place on the Mets' all-time list for career RBIs. Which former Met is ahead of him?
2. Which Mets third baseman led the NL with 38 home runs in 1991?
3. Which Mets third baseman was the NL MVP when he played for the Cardinals?
4. Which member of the Miracle Mets was known as The Glider or The Poet?
5. Which Mets third baseman is married to famed golfer Nancy Lopez?
6. This third baseman played against his brother, a Yankees third baseman, in the 1964 World Series.

7. Which infielder (not on this list) came over from the Dodgers and started for the Mets at both second and third base in the team's first two seasons, 1962 and 1963?
   a. Cliff Cook
   b. Charlie Neal
   c. Eddie Kasko
   d. Alex Grammas
8. Which retired Brooklyn Dodgers third baseman (who was also a former major league manager) was a coach on the original Mets?
   a. Cookie Lavagetto
   b. Joe Stripp
   c. Ransom Jackson
   d. Billy Cox
9. Who hit the first home run at Citi Field in 2009?
10. Which Mets third baseman was traded from the Mets to the Cardinals for Ken Boyer and then from the Cardinals to the Yankees for Roger Maris?
    a. Len Randle
    b. Charley Smith
    c. Gene Freese
    d. Harry Steinfeldt

Answers
1. Darryl Strawberry (733 RBIs as a Met)
2. Howard Johnson
3. Ken Boyer
4. Ed Charles
5. Ray Knight
6. Ken Boyer
7. b. Charlie Neal
8. a. Cookie Lavagetto
9. David Wright
10. b. Charley Smith

Five

Left Field

The Rankings!
1. Cleon Jones
2. Kevin McReynolds
3. George Foster
4. Cliff Floyd
5. Dave Kingman
6. Frank Thomas
7. Bernard Gilkey
8. Steve Henderson
9. Tommy Davis
10. Benny Agbayani

The Mets are pretty solid all the way down at this position. Jones was the team's first big star and McReynolds produced impressive power numbers in the late '80s and early '90s.

Foster was a disappointment, but he still gave the Mets some offense before he seemed to lose his focus, and Floyd was productive wherever he went when he wasn't injured.

Unfortunately, he was often injured. Kingman, of course, gave the team plenty of power but little else.

Thomas was the big bat in the lineup in the Mets' inaugural year, and Gilkey was a talented outfielder who had one great year with the team. Henderson started on some bad ballclubs, and he could hit but didn't provide much power. Davis had been great with the Dodgers, but a horrific ankle injury really altered his career, and he wasn't the same T.D. by the time he came to the Mets. Agbayani was a sometimes starter and a crowd favorite who was a reliable option when the Mets needed him.

Cleon Jones

After years of Mets fans following prospects in the minor leagues, two of those young players finally made the impact in the majors they'd been waiting for. Those same two players would go on to help lead the team to two pennants, including the Miracle Mets championship of 1969.

Cleon Jones was installed as the regular center fielder in '66, and a year later Bud Harrelson became the starting shortstop. Their arrival signaled the beginning of a new era for the team.

Add developing young pitchers Tom Seaver and Jerry Koosman, plus trades for catcher Jerry Grote and Tommie Agee, and the nucleus was there. The stage was set for the Miracle.

Jones was the Mets' first star position player, manning center field until he moved over to left when his childhood friend Agee arrived from the White Sox in '68. He's still among the all-time leaders for the team in many offensive categories, but we'll get to those later. We want to focus on '69, which was a landmark year for all of Metdom, and a big year for Jones. He was involved in a few significant events that came to define the season.

He had a blazing first half of the season, hitting .341 with 10 homers and 56 RBIs, which earned him the start in left field for the NL All-Star team. He also got two hits in the NL's 9–3 victory. Cleon finished the season—his best ever in the majors—hitting .340, one of the highest batting averages in Mets history, with an OBP of .422. He also socked 12 home runs, scored 92 runs, stole 16 bases, and knocked in 75, a career high.

But Cleon is best remembered for three things in '69: being removed from a game on July 30, possibly getting hit by a pitch in Game 5 of the World Series, and catching the final out for the Mets to win the title.

Let's set the scene for the July 30 incident.

The Mets were in second place, five games behind the Cubs, and the Astros came to New York for a doubleheader. The Mets were slaughtered 16–3 in the first game, and they were trailing 7–0 in the second game, when Johnny Edwards hit a double in Jones' direction in left field to make the score 8–0.

And then Mets manager Gil Hodges came out of the dugout and walked right past the infielders to where Cleon was standing in left. He was not happy that Jones didn't hustle after the ball. He spoke to his left fielder for a moment and then walked back to the dugout with Jones a few paces behind. Hodges sent Ron Swoboda out to play left field.

Though the official reason for the substitution was a leg injury, Jones was held out of a few more games, and it was later revealed that he was removed for a lack of hustle. Hodges decided to take his player out in a very public way to show that he would not tolerate lackadaisical play, even from his best player.

This move by Hodges is often cited as the turning point in the season because of the fear the skipper supposedly instilled in the entire team.

The Mets went on a tear and went 39–11 the rest of the way to finish eight games ahead of the Cubs.

Cleon Jones in '69

Jones finished third in the league in batting behind Pete Rose and Roberto Clemente and was second on the team to Tommie Agee in home runs, RBIs, and runs scored.

"In 1969 Cleon was our first real star," said veteran scribe Mike Shalin. "He never had another season like that, but it didn't matter, because he helped give us the ultimate gift."

In the Mets' three-game sweep of the Braves in the NLCS, Jones batted .429, which included a home run and three ribbies in the Mets' 11–6 win over the Braves in Game 2.

In the World Series against the heavily favored Orioles, the Mets had a 3 games to 1 lead, but the O's were ahead 3–0 in Game 5. Jones, leading off the sixth inning, was hit on the foot by a Dave McNally pitch, but umpire Lou DiMuro didn't see it that way, saying the ball didn't hit Jones. Hodges went to the plate to argue and showed the ump the shoe polish smudge on the ball.

That, apparently, was all DiMuro needed to see. He reversed his call. The next batter, Donn Clendenon, hit a two-run homer. Al Weis then smashed a solo home run in the seventh to tie the game. Jones doubled to lead off the eighth, before scoring on Swoboda's double.

The Mets were ahead 5–3 in the ninth when Davey Johnson hit a soft fly ball that Jones caught to give the Mets the World Series title.

"No Met fan will ever forget Cleon going down on one knee to catch that ball," Mike Shalin said.

In 1973 Jones helped the Mets to the World Series by getting three hits and two RBIs against the Reds in the NLCS final game.

By the time the Mets sent Cleon to the White Sox in '76, he led (or was second or third) in most of the team's career records. Thirty-five years later, he is still fourth in career at-bats, hits, and triples; seventh in runs; eighth in RBIs; and ninth in doubles.

Frank Thomas

Let's start this section off with a trivia question. (The answer should be obvious.)

In the New York Giants' last game at the Polo Grounds in 1957, the man who made the final out was the same slugger who would go on to hit the first home run for the Mets at the Polo Grounds in 1962. Who was that slugger?

Of course, the answer is Frank Thomas—the original Frank Thomas. "The Big Donkey," as he was known, who replaced Ralph

Kiner as the Pirates slugger in the '50s and then batted cleanup for the original Mets in '62, belting 34 home runs in that year of 120 defeats.

Not to be confused with "The Big Hurt" Frank Thomas of the White Sox (and soon Cooperstown), we're talking about the other Frank Thomas, who has been largely forgotten despite having a fine 16-year career in the National League.

The starting left fielder, who also played a little first and third base, was acquired by the Mets prior to their first season. He led the team in most offensive categories that first year, including home runs, RBIs, hits, runs, doubles, games played, and hit by pitches. It was an eventful year for Thomas.

In April '62, Thomas became the first major leaguer to get hit by two pitches in the same inning. And in August he set a record by hitting a total of six home runs in three consecutive games. During that stretch he hit seven homers in four games, with nine hits, and 12 RBIs.

On August 1, he hit two homers—including a grand slam—and drove in six runs, but the Mets lost the game 11–9. He had five multi–home run games during the season.

Thomas has warm memories of the 2½ seasons he played for the Mets before being sent to the Phillies in '64.

He reflected on that first Mets season with the blog Centerfield Maz. "We had a great ballclub," Thomas said. "We just didn't have any pitchers. We scored a lot of runs, but we lost a bunch of games in the seventh, eighth, and ninth innings. If we could have had a closer like they have today, we might have been in the thick of a pennant race."

He loved playing in New York and playing for Casey Stengel. Thomas roomed with future Hall of Famer Richie Ashburn on the road. They had also roomed together when they were teammates on the Cubs in '60 and '61.

Thomas came to the majors in '51 and eventually took over the Pirates' slugger's role when Kiner was traded to the Cubs in '53. In his first full season Thomas hit 30 home runs and drove in 102 runs.

In his career, The Big Donkey knocked in at least 80 runs six times, and more than 100 twice. He topped the 20–home run mark 10 times, with a high of 35 in '58. Thomas was the starting third baseman in the '58 All-Star Game.

After the Cincinnati fans stuffed the ballot box in '57, the voting was given to the players, coaches, and managers. "I relished the '58 game because I was voted in by my peers," said Thomas. "I think that age will always go down as the greatest era in baseball history."

Besides being a renowned slugger, and a wholesome family man (he didn't smoke or drink, and he and his wife had eight children), Thomas was also known for his versatility and his eagerness to play anywhere that would help the team.

He played all the outfield positions as well as third base and first base during his 16-year major league career.

"I was definitely versatile," he said. "I was probably a better outfielder than I was an infielder. But I made myself a good infielder and the managers appreciated that."

There's one more bit of history that involved Thomas. On June 8, 1961, Thomas was a member of the Milwaukee Braves. In the seventh inning, Hall of Famer Eddie Mathews came up and smacked a home run. Home run king Hank Aaron followed and did likewise. Joe Adcock followed, and the result was the same. Then Thomas came up and proceeded to deposit the ball in the seats at Crosley Field, marking the first time that one team had ever hit four consecutive home runs.

**Quiz!**

1. Which member of this list once hit 52 home runs as a member of an NL team other than the Mets?

2. Who set a Mets record with 44 doubles in 1996?

3. Which left fielder came to the Mets from the Reds in the Tom Seaver trade?

4. Who led the Mets with a career-high 34 home runs in 2005?

5. Who won one of his two NL home run crowns as a Met with 37 home runs in 1982?

6. Which Mets left fielder was a two-time NL batting champ in the early 1960s?

7. Who drove in more than 80 runs for the Mets in four straight years beginning in 1987?

8. Who led the NL in RBIs with 153 in 1962?

9. Which Met was an All-City basketball player at Boys High School in New York and a high school teammate of pro All-Star player and coach Lenny Wilkens?

10. Which Mets player was the NL starter in left field in the 1969 All-Star Game?

Answers
1. George Foster
2. Bernard Gilkey
3. Steve Henderson
4. Cliff Floyd
5. Dave Kingman
6. Tommy Davis
7. Kevin McReynolds
8. Tommy Davis
9. Tommy Davis
10. Cleon Jones

Six

Center Field

The Rankings!
1. Carlos Beltran
2. Tommie Agee
3. Mookie Wilson
4. Lenny Dykstra
5. Lee Mazzilli
6. Jim Hickman
7. Jay Payton
8. Lance Johnson
9. Richie Ashburn
10. Willie Mays

No other Mets center fielder reached the heights that Carlos Beltran reached during his good years with the Mets. That's why he gets the nod over Mets favorites Agee, Wilson, and Dykstra, all of whom were important cogs in one of the Mets two World Series championships. Mazzilli is a local boy and still a crowd favorite, and while he had some pretty good years on some pretty bad Mets teams, he never produced as expected when the Mets made him their first pick in the 1973 amateur draft.

A lot was expected of Hickman in the early Mets days, and it was frustrating watching him fall short of his potential. But he did give the Cubs some pretty good years after he left the Mets. Payton and Unser were serviceable flychasers, while Ashburn and Mays joined the team at the very end of their Hall of Fame careers. There are probably others who are worthy of these two spots, but you can't ignore Ashburn, nor Willie Mays, who is still the greatest player of the second half of the 20th century, and maybe of all time.

A long time ago, when there were discussions about who was the greatest ever, it was always a contest between Ty Cobb and Babe Ruth, with many giving the nod to Ruth because, early in his career, he was also one of the best pitchers in the game. Every once in a while some baseball historian would throw in the name Honus Wagner, and Joe DiMaggio fans will not give in if you say that Joltin' Joe was not No. 1 at anything. But in recent years, popular opinion is shifting toward Mays, probably the most exciting player to watch and the guy who could beat you in every way imaginable.

Willie has taken a lot of heat for staying around too long after his skills diminished, but, say hey, he was giving everybody more chances to watch Willie Mays play ball. And that was a treat, even during his final two—admittedly rough—seasons with the Mets. It was great to have him back where he belonged.

Carlos Beltran

Very quietly, Carlos Beltran has been one of the best players in baseball over the past dozen years or so.

In 2011, the Mets parted ways with the 34-year-old former All-Star. Beltran's expiring contract, combined with the Mets' financial problems, their slim playoff hopes, and the fact that Beltran's lucrative seven-year contract was expiring at the end of the season, forced the Mets to trade the switch-hitting outfielder to the contending Giants.

Though he has an impressive postseason record—a .366 batting average with 11 home runs and eight stolen bases in eight tries—his image has been defined by one single at-bat, when he looked at a called third strike to end the 2006 NLCS against the Cardinals.

Ironically, that came after Beltran produced one of the greatest seasons in Mets history. That season, Beltran hit .275 with an OBP of .388. He drove in 116 runs, his 127 runs scored set a Mets single-season record, and his 41 homers tied a single-season record. He started in the All-Star Game and hit three grand slams in July (a team record). He won the Silver Slugger Award.

Beltran was also outstanding on defense. He had a .995 fielding percentage, making only two errors in 372 chances while registering 13 outfield assists on his way to winning the Gold Gove Award. He finished fourth in the MVP voting that year, and he was outstanding in the NLCS before that unfortunate at-bat.

Beltran continued to produce at that all-star level on both offense and defense in both '07 and '08. The next two seasons, though, were cut short by injuries. Beltran returned in '11 and moved to right field to make it a little easier on his arthritic knees, which had undergone several surgeries. Production-wise he was back to his old self, leading the Mets in games played, home runs, and RBIs, and once again contributing fine defense.

"Now that I feel 100 percent, I'm looking forward to playing my game the way I want to—getting on base, stealing bases, and trying to help the team any way I can," said Beltran.

And then, on May 13, almost as a farewell to loyal Mets fans, Beltran had one of the great nights of his career against the Rockies. He hit three home runs for the first time in his career, two from the left side of the plate and one from the right side, with a career-high six RBIs. It was his 17th multi-homer game as a Met, which ties him with Mike Piazza for second place in Mets history. Darryl Strawberry is the leader with 22.

"I've never seen a day like that before," Mets manager Terry Collins said to Adam Gross of MetsOnline.

"Being able to do something like this, I felt like a little kid, honestly," Beltran told Gross. "I was smiling. I never smile a lot. But I was smiling."

For his career, as of this writing, Beltran has hit 295 home runs with 1,128 RBIs, he has scored 1,167 runs, and he's stolen 292 bases. He has a .282 career batting average and a .361 OBP. He's made the All-Star team six times. Beltran has had 100 or more RBIs eight times and 100 or more runs seven times.

"I've said all along, Carlos is the most gifted baseball player I've ever seen," said former teammate Johnny Damon.

Tommie Agee

Tommie Agee gave the Mets the best years of his knees.

In the championship season of 1969 and then again the following year, Agee played through the pain and showed New York fans how good the outfielder from Alabama could have been, even though he always played in pain.

Agee came up with the White Sox and won the AL Rookie of the Year Award and Gold Glove in '66. After a down year, the Sox traded him to the Mets for four players.

His Mets career got off to a discouraging start when, on the first pitch of Grapefruit League play, Bob Gibson beaned Agee and sent him to the hospital.

Early in the season, Agee went on a nightmarish 0–34 slump that dropped his average to .102, and it didn't get much better as the season went on and he finished with a .217 batting average, five home runs, and only 17 RBIs.

In spite of that, manager Gil Hodges installed him in the leadoff spot because he wanted a leadoff hitter with both speed and power. Hodges had faith that his center fielder could pull out of the hitting doldrums, so there was Agee in center field and leading off again on Opening Day in '69.

This time Agee began to repay the manager's confidence in him with a fast start that included knocking in the first runs of the season with a three-run double. Then, two days later, he hit two home runs in a game, the first of which was a true tape-measure blast into the upper deck in left field.

"I've never seen a ball hit like that," said on-deck hitter Rod Gaspar to writer John Vorperian for SABR's The Baseball Biography Project. "Just incredible."

The man who threw the pitch, Larry Jaster of the Expos, reported that Agee hit the ball "almost like a golf ball."

Agee went on to provide the offensive and defensive leadership as the Mets later caught and passed the Cubs with an amazing second-half run that included an impressive 41–23 record in one-run games. He finished the season with 26 home runs and 76 RBIs.

Agee's outfield partner and good friend Cleon Jones was also enjoying his best season, and he gives Agee some credit for his success as well. "I had a great year because of him," Jones told Vorperian. "There weren't many people getting on base, but he was. And he made us a good defensive team. We didn't have a whole lot of offense, but we didn't beat ourselves. He made the difference defensively."

The Mets overtook the Cubs and won the pennant by eight games, finishing with a 100–62 record.

Agee had two homers, four RBIs, and hit .357 as the Mets breezed by the Braves in three games in baseball's first league championship playoff. They then met the Orioles, who were big favorites, in the World Series. As it turned out, he was saving the best for last, helping to put the final touches on the Miracle.

In Game 3, with the Series tied at 1–1, Agee had what *Sports Illustrated* called "the most spectacular World Series game that any center fielder has ever enjoyed."

In the first inning, Agee led off with a home run off future Hall of Famer Jim Palmer that turned out to be the game winner in the 5–0 Mets victory, behind the combined four-hit pitching of Gary Gentry and Nolan Ryan.

But it was Agee's play in the field that made him a Mets legend. He made two of the most incredible catches this side of Willie Mays, saving what was possibly five Oriole runs from crossing the plate.

The O's were ahead 3–0 in the top of the fourth, with runners on first and third and two outs. Elrod Hendricks, the Orioles' catcher, hit a Gentry pitch to left-center. It looked like it was headed into the gap for extra bases. Agee reached out and grabbed the ball backhanded. It landed in his glove's webbing plainly visible as Agee crashed into the wall at the 396-foot sign.

As Agee headed back to the wall in left-center, left fielder Jones was confident his buddy would make the catch. "I saw him pound his fist into the glove," Jones said. "Whenever he got ready to make a catch, he would pound his fist into his glove."

Then, in the Baltimore seventh, with the bases loaded and Ryan now on the mound for the Mets, Paul Blair slammed a drive to deep right-center, and Agee again sprinted after the ball, this time going to his left. When he got to the warning track, he just dove for the ball like a swimmer coming off the blocks and made the catch as he landed flat on the ground with his arm outstretched.

"I thought I might get it without diving," said Agee. "But the wind dropped the ball straight down and I had to hit the dirt."

The Shea Stadium crowd gave Agee a standing ovation when he came up to lead off the bottom of the seventh.

"Words can't describe how that made me feel," Agee said. "I felt like I wanted to hit two home runs in that one time at bat." He walked.

Reporters immediately compared the catch off the Blair blast, which saved a sure triple and possibly an inside-the-park homer, with other great World Series catches, such as Willie Mays' catch off Vic Wertz in 1954 and Sandy Amoros robbing Yogi Berra in '55.

After the Series, Agee won the *Sporting News* NL Comeback Player of the Year Award.

In 1970, Agee won his second Gold Glove and had another fine year, hitting 24 home runs with 75 RBIs and a .286 average. But after that the chronic knee injuries began to take their toll, and the Mets traded Agee to the Astros after the '72 season. He retired the following year.

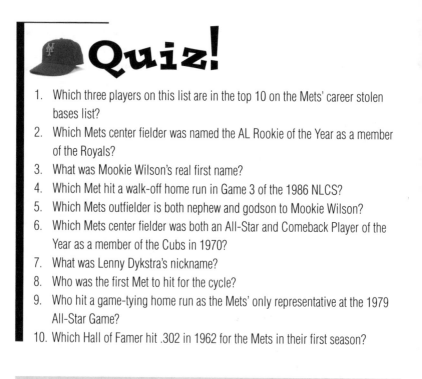

Quiz!

1. Which three players on this list are in the top 10 on the Mets' career stolen bases list?

2. Which Mets center fielder was named the AL Rookie of the Year as a member of the Royals?

3. What was Mookie Wilson's real first name?

4. Which Met hit a walk-off home run in Game 3 of the 1986 NLCS?

5. Which Mets outfielder is both nephew and godson to Mookie Wilson?

6. Which Mets center fielder was both an All-Star and Comeback Player of the Year as a member of the Cubs in 1970?

7. What was Lenny Dykstra's nickname?

8. Who was the first Met to hit for the cycle?

9. Who hit a game-tying home run as the Mets' only representative at the 1979 All-Star Game?

10. Which Hall of Famer hit .302 in 1962 for the Mets in their first season?

Answers

1. Lee Mazzilli (5th with 152), Lenny Dykstra (7th with 116), and Carlos Beltran (9th with 100)
2. Carlos Beltran
3. William
4. Lenny Dykstra
5. Preston Wilson
6. Jim Hickman
7. Nails
8. Jim Hickman
9. Lee Mazzilli
10. Richie Ashburn

Seven

Right Field

The Rankings!
1. Darryl Strawberry
2. Rusty Staub
3. Shawn Green
4. Bobby Bonilla
5. Joel Youngblood
6. Ron Swoboda
7. Art Shamsky
8. Roger Cedeno
9. Jeff Francoeur
10. Ellis Valentine

Okay, so top to bottom this is not as good as the Yankees' right field, but there are some pretty fair thumpers at the top in Strawberry and Staub.

If Strawberry had fulfilled his potential he would be headed to the Hall of Fame, but despite the fact that he had some pretty great years for the Mets, it was not to be. Staub was a solid hitter who played 23 seasons and is one of those players who is just short of Cooperstown.

Then there's a drop-off to Green and Bonilla, neither of whom had his best years with the Mets, but who both had some good stretches in New York.

Youngblood was a pretty fair ballplayer on some bad Mets teams, while Swoboda and Shamsky gave Gil Hodges a great platooning duo in 1969. The others are just filling out the list.

Darryl Strawberry

There were only a few players since World War II whose very presence in the batter's box was an event. You actually looked forward to them coming to the plate. Darryl Strawberry was one of these players, right up until his final days with the Yankees in 1999. The others who come to mind are Ted Williams, Willie Mays, Mickey Mantle, Jackie Robinson, and Frank "The Big Hurt" Thomas. The first four are in the Hall of Fame, and Thomas will get there soon.

There was just a certain something about the manner, the stance, and the swing that made you sure you were going to see something exciting happen. There were other great players, but they didn't have that certain something that commanded you to sit and watch the game at least through this at-bat, even if it wasn't a particularly crucial part of the game. And if it was an important situation, you just knew Darryl was going to come through, although I'm sure I saw him fan on a number of these occasions.

Right from the beginning, Strawberry was unique because we were all aware of him when he was a high school player. In those days you rarely heard anything about high school or college players, so when we started to read about this teenage sensation and news reports on this super prospect we only hoped that he would someday play for the Mets.

The Mets drafted him with the first pick of the 1980 draft, and a new era in Mets history was about to begin. And to a great extent Strawberry met our expectations. He was The Man in the Mets' lineup for almost a decade, and he helped lead the team to the '86 World Series.

He became famous for his high-arching home runs, called "moonshots," and often showed that he could someday be mentioned in the same breath with those aforementioned superstars.

But a career-long battle with drug and alcohol problems, health and injury issues, legal problems, and sometimes what appeared to be indifference, kept him from rising to the heights that everyone expected. While he was still the most popular player in New York with the Mets and later with the Yankees, where he contributed to three more titles, Strawberry's career was a series of interruptions that disappointed fans. These, along with ace pitcher Dwight Gooden's problems, kept the Mets from being one of the most dominating teams in baseball through the '90s.

Strawberry was named Rookie of the Year in '83 after hitting 26 home runs and driving in 74 runs. He made the All-Star team eight straight times after his rookie season, but even during the successful years his attitude could irritate his teammates and his manager.

Davey Johnson, who was Strawberry's manager for seven seasons, told Mike Puma of ESPN.com that the slugger was comfortable hitting 30 homers a season and stealing 30 bases, even when he could have accomplished more.

"He had the swing, the grace, the power," Johnson said. "When he wanted to be, he was as good as it gets."

"He can be the most exciting player in the game when he feels like it," said teammate Mackey Sasser. "The situation is whether or not he feels like it."

Strawberry slides safely into second during the legendary Game 6—Flushing, New York, October 25, 1986.

Despite his off-field troubles, Strawberry's time with the Mets was the team's most successful period in its 50-year history, and he was at the center of a team that finished either first or second every year between '84 and '90.

The '86 team that won the World Series won 108 games during the season and is regarded as one of the strongest teams of all time. Darryl smashed 27 homers and drove in 93 runs during the season, and he came through with a pair of homers in the NLCS against the Astros, and another homer in the historic World Series against Boston.

His best year was '87, when he led the NL with 39 homers and drove in 104 runs. He also batted a career-high .284. That year Strawberry became the first NL player to be elected to the All-Star team in each of his first four seasons. In '88, he came up big again with 39 home runs and 101 RBIs and finished second to Kirk Gibson of the Dodgers in the MVP voting. The Mets, though favored in the NLCS, were beaten by the Dodgers in seven games.

Despite an arrest for domestic battery and a stint in an alcohol facility, Strawberry had another big year in '90 with 37 homers and a Mets-record 108 RBIs.

After signing a five-year contract with the Dodgers, Strawberry came through with 28 homers his first year, but he was hampered by back injuries that wiped out a good part of the next two years. In '94, he was released by the Dodgers after admitting to a substance abuse problem and going into the Betty Ford Center for treatment for 28 days. In the off-season, Strawberry and his agent were indicted on tax evasion charges for failing to report income from baseball card and autograph shows. He was later suspended by baseball for 60 days for testing positive for cocaine.

In '95 the outfielder signed with the Yankees in July, had moderate success, and participated in the ALCS that year. He saw limited action in '96 but stepped up big in the ALCS with three homers and a .417 average, as the Yankees won their first championship in 18 years.

To prove that with Darryl Strawberry it was always something, he missed most of '97 with a knee injury, but he came back in '98 to hit 24 homers and help the Yankees to the playoffs. He didn't play in the postseason because he was diagnosed with colon cancer and underwent surgery.

The Yankees dedicated their World Series win over the Padres to Strawberry.

In '99, he was arrested in Tampa for cocaine possession and for soliciting an undercover officer for sex. He later received another baseball suspension for testing positive for cocaine, and he underwent further cancer surgery during his suspension.

In '01, he became suicidal after another drug episode and spent time in a hospital and then in a drug treatment center. He was ousted from the drug treatment center for breaking the rules and was sentenced to prison for violating his probation. He served 11 months.

Despite all of his problems, Strawberry is loved in New York for his service to both teams.

He hit nine home runs with 22 RBIs in 40 postseason games, and his team won eight series out of 10. He had two three-home run games in his career and is one of only five players in history to hit two pinch-hit grand slams in the same season.

In recent years, Strawberry has served as host of the Mets pre- and postgame shows on SNY, he's opened a restaurant, and he frequently donates money to and makes appearances at charity events.

Looking back on the problems and the missed opportunities to take his place among the game's greats, Strawberry said, "I'm not ashamed of who I am. Of course I'm ashamed for the things [that] have happened. But with life experiences, you're able to give back and help others."

Rusty Staub

I've always maintained that if the Mets could have held on to their prospects of the late '60s and early '70s, namely Nolan Ryan, Amos Otis, and Ken Singleton, they could have stayed among the contenders throughout the decade.

And when I say that, someone usually reminds me that the Mets received Rusty Staub when they traded Singleton and two others to the Expos in 1972, and without Staub, who gave the Mets nine good years, the team would never have won the '73 NL pennant.

"Le Grand Orange," as Montreal fans named Staub during a three-year stay north of the border, is surely one of the most underrated players of all time and is certainly worthy of Hall of Fame consideration. His No. 10 was the first number retired by the Expos organization.

A six-time All-Star, Staub retired after 23 seasons in the majors with 2,716 hits, 292 home runs, 499 doubles, and 1,466 RBIs. Staub batted .300 five times. There aren't too many players with those credentials who have failed to make it to the Hall of Fame.

He was also a smart hitter who knew the strike zone. He had a .279 lifetime average, an OBP of .362, and he never struck out more than 58 times in a season. Even though he wasn't the speediest flychaser, he was great in the field and had a strong, accurate arm.

"Rusty knew how to play the game," said Tim McCarver. "He was a good all-around player. He was a very good offensive player when he was older and a very good defensive player when he was younger."

After helping the Mets get to the '73 playoffs (15 HR, 76 RBIs, .279 BA) Staub was a bright star, displaying his talents in his only trip to the postseason. He had three home runs and five RBIs in the NLCS victory over the Reds and made a spectacular catch that robbed Dan Driessen of an extra-base hit in the 11th inning of Game 4. That resulted in Staub injuring his right shoulder, causing him to have to throw underhanded in the World Series.

In the Mets' seven-game loss to the A's in the Fall Classic, Staub hit .423, socked one home run, and drove in six runs.

In the '75 season, Staub became the first Met ever to reach 100 RBIs. He knocked in 105, a team record until it was tied by Gary Carter and later broken by Darryl Strawberry and then Howard Johnson.

"He was a situational type hitter who knew what to look for, when to look for it, how to look for it in situations," said Lee Mazzilli. "I always felt he was going to hit the ball hard somewhere."

When he left the Mets, Staub starred for the Tigers for four years and eventually returned to the Mets for five more seasons, when he became one of the great pinch-hitters. In 1983 he tied the NL record with eight consecutive pinch-hits.

He also tied a major league record with 25 pinch-hit RBIs and *set* a major league record of 81 pinch-hit appearances.

"You talk about the student of hitting," said Joe Torre. "With Rusty there was no question, this was a science for him. He was a good hitter."

Quiz!

1. Which player on this list is one of three people in history to hit major league home runs when they were teenagers *and* when they were in their forties?
2. Darryl Strawberry was the NL Rookie of the Year in 1983. Who won the AL award that year?
3. Who was the NL Rookie of the Year in 1984?
4. Who is the only player to have at least 500 hits with four different teams?
5. Which right fielder was nicknamed "Rocky"?

6. Which Mets right fielder, in his early days in the league, was part of a great young Pirates outfield with Barry Bonds and Andy Van Slyke?

7. Which Mets right fielder retired after the 2007 season with career totals of 328 home runs and 1,071 RBIs?

8. Which Met managed a team in Israel when his playing days were over?

9. Which Mets right fielder won a Gold Glove with the Expos in 1978 and is considered to have one of the greatest arms of any outfielder in baseball history?

10. The character Robert on *Everybody Loves Raymond* had a dog named after which Mets right fielder?

    a. Swoboda

    b. Shamsky

    c. Strawberry

    d. Youngblood

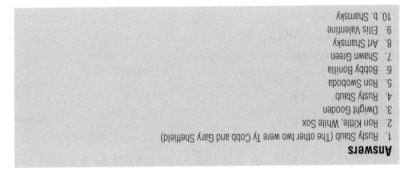

Answers

1. Rusty Staub (The other two were Ty Cobb and Gary Sheffield)
2. Ron Kittle, White Sox
3. Dwight Gooden
4. Rusty Staub
5. Ron Swoboda
6. Bobby Bonilla
7. Shawn Green
8. Art Shamsky
9. Ellis Valentine
10. b. Shamsky

Eight

Catcher

The Rankings!
1. Mike Piazza
2. Gary Carter
3. Jerry Grote
4. Todd Hundley
5. John Stearns
6. Paul Lo Duca
7. Ron Hodges
8. Ramon Castro
9. Duffy Dyer
10. Mackey Sasser

The top six people on this list have a total of 35 All-Star selections in their careers. Of course, Piazza and Carter have 23 of those, but the next four were very good starters at the position.

Piazza has been called the greatest-hitting catcher of all time, and his career .308 BA, 427 home runs, and 1,335 RBIs would support that statement. He was also Rookie of the Year in 1993, won 10 Silver Slugger Awards, and was the MVP of the 1996 All-Star Game. Hitting was Piazza's strength, and he was considered average or below in all other aspects of the position.

Carter, on the other hand, doesn't have Mike's numbers, but he was a productive hitter his whole career, batting .262 with 324 home runs and 1,225 RBIs, not to mention five Silver Sluggers. He also won three Gold Gloves. Carter was considered an excellent handler of pitchers and he had an above-average arm. He was the All Star Game MVP twice, in 1981 and '84. He was inducted into the baseball Hall of Fame in 2003.

Grote was one of the best defensive catchers in the game during the late 1960s, and he led the Mets pitching staff to a championship in '69. Hundley was a slugger who just happened to play catcher. He set the Mets' single-season home run record when he hit 41 in '96.

Stearns was another hard-nosed leader type who could beat you in a number of ways, including on the basepaths, and Lo Duca gave the Mets a good number-two man in the batting order when he came over in '06.

Hodges, Castro, Dyer, and Sasser were reliable backstops who could be trusted to fill the starting job for extended periods when they were needed.

John Stearns

In recent years we've been reading that former Mets catcher John Stearns doesn't want to be known by the nickname that so vividly described his style of play as a major league baseball player and before that as an all-conference defensive back on some fine Colorado teams.

"Bad Dude" Stearns, who has been a longtime coach, scout, and executive with several teams, is hoping to get back to the majors as a manager, and he doesn't believe that the Bad Dude image is appropriate for a dignified authority figure. Or is it? We can remember making up nicknames a lot worse than that for our bosses.

We've loved Bad Dude and the image it conjured up going back to the Colorado days when he was so good that he was drafted by the Buffalo Bills of the NFL.

"It worked for me as a player," Stearns told Irv Moss of the *Denver Post* a few years ago. "There's no hiding the fact that when I was young, I lacked humility. I built a reputation of being a cocky, arrogant player. That reputation is hard to live down."

But he chose to play baseball when the Phillies picked him No. 2 overall in the amateur draft, ahead of future Hall of Famers Robin Yount and Dave Winfield.

Because we were such big Stearns fans in the old days, we're going to resurrect The Bad Dude just for this discussion of our choice for the No. 5 best Mets catcher of all time.

Let's look back on his well-earned Bad Dude resume in baseball to see if you agree.

He was certainly a hard-nosed player who provided toughness and skills on a series of Mets teams that were among the worst ever. And the fans loved him.

In 1977, when he topped the team with 25 doubles and tied for the lead with 12 home runs, Stearns became annoyed by the Braves mascot Chief Noc-A-Homa and chased him from the field before a game. The following year, Stearns put a tag on Pirates great Dave Parker that broke the outfielder's cheekbone. Parker had recently run over two other catchers, but he wasn't smart to barrel into the former All-Star safety.

In '79 Stearns collided with the Expos' Gary Carter at home plate when Carter tried to score from first on a throwing error.

Stearns believed Carter threw an elbow at home plate and the two started fighting. Both benches and bullpens emptied and both Carter and Stearns were ejected.

In '80, a pair of drunken fans jumped onto the field and the police couldn't catch them. But Stearns ran from behind the plate to the third-base side of the infield and tackled one of them.

On July 4, 1980, rookie Expos pitcher Bill Gullickson threw a pitch over the head of Met Mike Jorgensen, who had been the victim of a terrible beanball injury the previous season with the Rangers. Jorgensen just motioned to Gullickson, as Stearns, who wasn't even playing, ran out of the dugout to the mound and bodyslammed the pitcher to the ground.

In his 11 seasons in the majors (10 with the Mets) Stearns batted .260, hit 46 home runs, and drove in 312 runs. He was also good for about 65 walks and 18 stolen bases a year.

In '78, his best year, he belted 15 homers and had 73 RBIs and 25 stolen bases, which was a record for a catcher. He was also outstanding on defense. He was just unfortunate to arrive in New York during the Mets' down years. But he was one of the bright spots, and the fans loved their Bad Dude.

"I've been trying to get rid of it for about 30 years," Stearns said with a laugh. "I heard the phrase 'Bad Dude' back in 1970. I used it when I was talking to a writer from *Sports Illustrated*. The guy nicknamed me 'Bad Dude' and I couldn't get rid of it."

Jerry Grote

And speaking of bad dudes, we give you Jerry Grote, the Mets' catcher for 12 years, including the Miracle Mets championship year. Grote preceded Stearns as the starting catcher, and the two were teammates for three seasons.

Grote, a two-time All-Star and Mets' team leader, was so great on defense and handling pitchers that Johnny Bench once said that "if Jerry Grote was on the Reds, I would be the third baseman."

He was also known as one of the most intense competitors of the day, a man who competed ferociously at anything, even board games.

Writer John Strubel told of an incident in 1976 during a backgammon game between Grote and rookie pitcher Bob Myrick. When he lost to the rookie, Grote exploded, sending the board and its pieces across the room with a single swing of his arm.

"I just sat there staring at him—hard," Myrick remembered. "He got up and picked up all the pieces, and we never had a cross word. He was a perfectionist."

Grote was so competitive and so eager to play the slightest advantage that one of his trademark moves was to roll the ball to the side of the pitcher's mound closest to the Mets' dugout when the inning ended with a strikeout, so the opposing pitcher would have to walk a little farther to pick up the ball.

According to Tom Seaver, Grote realized way back in spring training of 1969 that the Mets were capable of going all the way.

"Jerry said it because he knew the pitching," said Seaver to Anthony McCarron of the *New York Daily News*. "Seaver, Koosman, Ryan, Gentry. We had a whole stack of very good arms and he knew what that meant, and that's exactly what happened."

Grote knew the team was different in '69.

"We're a young team. We're just coming," he said at the beginning of the season as reported by writer Joseph Wancho in SABR's The Biography Project. "We all played together a few years. You get to know each other and things improve...There's more togetherness. There's more pride. We're a close-knit team."

And, as a tough taskmaster, Grote drove those pitchers to make sure they kept developing and fulfilled their potential.

"When I came up I was scared to death of him," said '72 Rookie of the Year Jon Matlack. "If you bounced a curveball in the dirt, he'd get mad. I worried about him more than the hitter."

"He could be trouble if you didn't do what he said," said former pitcher Craig Swan. "He wanted you to throw the pitches he called."

Grote was the commanding officer on the field and he constantly let the pitchers know that he was the boss.

The Mets got Grote in a trade with the Astros in '66, and he became the starting catcher upon his arrival. His defense and the way he handled young pitchers were noticed immediately.

In '68, he was chosen as the NL starting catcher in the All-Star Game and he finished the season with a .282 batting average.

Grote was in there almost every day during the chase for the pennant in '69. He drove in the winning run as the catcher for Seaver in a five-hitter one day, and then the next day he caught all 21 innings of a doubleheader sweep of the Expos.

The catcher had a .991 fielding percentage that year, and he had a 56.3 caught-stealing percentage that was second in the league. The young pitching staff he guided led the league in victories, shutouts, and was second in ERA. Grote was the catcher for all three games of the first NLCS ever played and every inning of the five-game World Series. In the Series, the Orioles' hitters were held to a .148 batting average.

Grote led the league's catchers in putouts and range factor in both '70 and '71. The next two years he missed major time with injuries. He had surgery to remove bone chips from his right elbow in '72. And then, in May '73, Grote went on the disabled list for two months because he broke a bone in his right arm when he was hit by a pitch.

But he returned in July to catch during the pennant race, and just as he had in '69, Grote caught every inning of the postseason:

an upset NLCS win over the Reds and a seven-game loss to the Athletics in the World Series.

He received his second All-Star nod in '74, but the injuries were starting to wear him down and he split the catching with Duffy Dyer that year. In '75, he had a career-high .295 batting average and led the league's catchers with a .995 fielding percentage.

For the profile of Grote in SABR's The Biography Project, Hall of Famer Lou Brock told Joseph Wancho, "For quickness in getting rid of the ball and accuracy, I have to pick Grote." Brock also said that when Grote was behind the plate, he tried to take bigger leads off first base and take advantage of the pitcher to give himself a chance.

Mike Piazza and Roger Clemens are kept apart by an umpire during Game 2 of the 2000 World Series.

1. Which Mets catcher's father was an All-Star catcher with the Cubs?
2. Who was the catcher who hit .306 for the Mets team that went to the playoffs in 2006?
3. Which catcher (not on this list) played for the Mets from 1963 to 1965 and came to the majors with the Yankees in 1960?
4. Which Mets catcher played his entire 12-year career, from 1973 to 1984, with the Mets, mostly as a backup?
5. Which catcher played briefly for the Mets and went on to manage the team?
6. Did Mike Piazza play more seasons as a Met or as a Dodger?
7. How many times did Gary Carter make the NL All-Star team?
8. Which Mets catcher (not on this list) was the Mets' first pick in the 1961 expansion draft?
9. Which Mets catcher was nicknamed "The Kid"?
10. Who was the Mets' backup catcher (not on this list) who went a perfect 3-for-3 at the plate in the postseason in 1969? It was the only time he ever played in the postseason.

Answers

1. Todd Hundley, whose father is Randy Hundley
2. Paul Lo Duca
3. Jesse Gonder
4. Ron Hodges
5. Yogi Berra
6. Piazza played eight seasons with the Mets and seven with the Dodgers.
7. 11 times
8. Hobie Landrith
9. Gary Carter
10. J.C. Martin

Nine

Pitcher

The Rankings!

Starters
1. Tom Seaver
2. Dwight Gooden
3. Jerry Koosman
4. David Cone
5. Ron Darling
6. Jon Matlack
7. Al Leiter
8. Johan Santana
9. Sid Fernandez
10. Tom Glavine
11. Steve Trachsel
12. Bob Ojeda
13. Pedro Martinez
14. Bret Saberhagen
15. Frank Viola
16. Nolan Ryan
17. Rick Reed
18. Bobby Jones
19. Craig Swan
20. Gary Gentry

Closers
1. John Franco
2. Jesse Orosco
3. Tug McGraw
4. Roger McDowell
5. Randy Myers
6. Armando Benitez
7. Ron Taylor
8. Neil Allen
9. Skip Lockwood
10. Francisco Rodriguez
H.M. Billy Wagner
H.M. Jeff Reardon

Ever since the mid- and late '60s, when prospects like Seaver, Koosman, Ryan, and McGraw joined up and helped the team to its first championship in '69, for the Mets it's always been about the pitching.

The Mets' pitching history includes a healthy number of homegrowns, such as the aforementioned, along with Gooden and Matlack, and imports such as Hall of Fame member Warren Spahn and future Hall of Famers Glavine and Martinez.

The Mets have usually had good pitchers, except during the dismal early '60s and late '70s. However, Mets pitchers' career numbers aren't that high, outside of Seaver, Gooden, and Koosman, because most of the top guys were in for only a limited time.

Even Seaver was traded to the Reds in 1977 and spent six years in Cincinnati. He came back to Shea for a year and then toiled the last three years of his career in Chicago (White Sox) and Boston.

Hall of Famer Tom Seaver throws a pitch in the 1969 World Series.

And Gooden, were it not for his personal problems, should have spent many more years pitching at the top of his game in New York, and he should have posted Hall of Fame numbers.

In 50 years, only Seaver, with 198 victories, Gooden with 157, and Koosman with 140, have triple-digit wins for the Mets. And the same three are the only pitchers who gave the team 2,000 innings or more.

But even when we couldn't always count on career Mets, the pitching has usually been there, and the savvy New York crowds have had the enjoyment of getting to see reliable starters who settled in for a while, such as Cone, Darling, Leiter, and Fernandez, or those who came by for what seemed like only a few moments, such as Saberhagen, Viola, and Orel Hershiser.

In addition, the Mets during their okay-to-great years usually had a reliable arm or two in the bullpen, which is why we included a dazzling dozen rather than merely a top 10.

Relievers are a transient bunch, so it may not be that impressive, but four of the all-time top 10 in career saves once served as Mets closers: Franco (424) is fourth, Wagner (422) is fifth, Reardon (367) is seventh, and Meyers (347) is ninth.

Plus, Aguilera, Isringhausen, Rodriguez, and Benitez are all in the top 30.

No-Hitters

Incredible as it may seem, there has never been a no-hitter thrown by a Mets pitcher. There have been five no-hitters pitched against the Mets, and many former or future Mets hurlers have thrown no-hitters as members of other teams, but the closest a Met has ever come was in '61 when Tom Seaver had a no-hitter going against the Cubs when Jimmy Qualls singled with one out in the ninth.

But we can salute the Mets alums and Mets-to-be for their achievements and we can acknowledge those who victimized the Mets with their outstanding no-hit performances.

So, here is the history of the no-hitters the Mets were involved in, either directly or indirectly.

After They Were Mets No-Hitters
Nolan Ryan

Any conversation about no-hitters has to begin with The Ryan Express, who holds the all-time record of having pitched seven no-hitters in his career.

Ryan came up with the Mets in '66 and played in five seasons before being traded to the Angels for Jim Fregosi after the '71 season. While a Met, Ryan had a record of 29–38, which included a 6–3 record in the championship season of '69. He posted a victory in the ALCS and pitched in the World Series before moving on to stardom for the Angels, Astros, and Rangers.

Ryan finished his 27-season career with 324 wins, an ERA of 3.19, and baseball's all-time strikeout record of 5,714. He was elected to the Hall of Fame in 1999.

Here's a rundown of his record seven no-hitters.

1. Ryan (Angels) 3–0 over the Royals, May 5, 1973
2. Ryan (Angels) 6–0 over the Athletics, July 15, 1973
3. Ryan (Angels) 4–0 over the Twins, September 28 1974
4. Ryan (Angels) 1–0 over the Orioles, June 1, 1975
5. Ryan (Astros) 5–0 over the Dodgers, September 26, 1981
6. Ryan (Rangers) 5–0 over the Athletics, June 11, 1990
7. Ryan (Rangers) 3–0 over the Blue Jays, May 1, 1991

Tom Seaver

This former Rookie of the Year ('67), three-time Cy Young Award winner ('69, '73, and '75), and five-time 20-game winner is the greatest player in Mets history and holds most of their pitching records. In his 12-year Mets career, Seaver was 198–124. His overall record is 311–205, and he's sixth on the all-time strikeout list with 3,640, and eighth on the all-time shutout list with 62. He was elected to the Hall of Fame in '93.

1. Seaver (Reds) 4–0 over the Cardinals, June 16, 1973

Mike Scott

Scott was a high draft pick who started with the Mets and had a record of 14–27 from 1970 to 1982. He was traded to the Astros and had much more success, especially after he mastered the split-finger fastball. In '86, Scott won the Cy Young Award and struck out 306 batters. He had a record of 110–81 in his nine years with the Astros.

1. Scott (Astros) 2–0 over the Giants, September 25, 1986

Dwight Gooden

Gooden was on his way to becoming one of the best pitchers of all time, with a Rookie of the Year Award ('84) and a Cy Young Award at age 20 in '85 (Triple Crown of pitching with 24–4 record, 1.53 ERA, and 268 strikeouts), but it never worked out quite that way after his initial success.

1. Gooden (Yankees) 2–0 over the Mariners, May 14, 1996

David Cone

Cone went a phenomenal 20–3 with the Mets in '88. He twice led the league in strikeouts and finished his seven-year Mets career with an 81–51 record. He was 194–126 during his 17-season career.

1. Cone (Yankees) 6–0 (perfect game) over the Expos, July 18, 1999

Before They Were Mets No-Hitters
Warren Spahn

At the age of 44, Hall of Famer Spahn had a 4–12 record for the Mets before moving on to the Giants to finish his career that year.

The lefty's lifetime record was 363–245 and he was a 20-game winner 13 times for the Braves. He was elected to the Hall of Fame in '73.

1. Spahn (Braves) 4–0 over the Phillies, September 16, 1960
2. Spahn (Braves) 1–0 over the Giants, April 28, 1961

Don Cardwell

The Mets received Cardwell in a trade with the Pirates after the '66 season. He pitched for the Mets for four years and had a 26–34 record, including an 8–10 mark in the championship year. He made one appearance in the World Series.

1. Cardwell (Cubs) 4–0 over the Cardinals, May 15, 1960

Dean Chance

This Cy Young Award winner (Angels '64) and two-time 20-game winner pitched briefly for the Mets in '70.

1. Chance (Twins) 2–1 over the Indians, August 25, 1967

Bret Saberhagen

Saberhagen is a two-time Cy Young Award winner ('85 and '89) and two-time 20-game winner. In '89 with the Royals, he was 23–6 with a 2.16 ERA. He was 29–21 with the Mets from 1992 to 1995.

1. Saberhagen (Royals) 7–0 over the White Sox, August 26, 1991

Al Leiter

Leiter pitched for the Mets for seven years and had a record of 95–67. Twice he pitched for them in the postseason. His career record was 162–132 over 19 seasons.

1. Leiter (Marlins) 11–0 over the Rockies, May 11, 1996

No-hitters against the Mets
There have been seven no-hitters pitched by opposing pitchers against the Mets.
1. Sandy Koufax (Dodgers), 5–0, June 30, 1962
2. Jim Bunning (Phillies) 6–0 (perfect game), June 21, 1964
3. Sandy Koufax (Dodgers) 1–0 (perfect game), September 9, 1965
4. Bob Moose (Pirates) 4–0, September 20, 1969
5. Bill Stoneman (Expos) 7–0, October 2, 1972
6. Ed Halicki (Giants) 6–0, August 24, 1975
7. Darryl Kile (Astros) 7–1, September 8, 1993

Tom Seaver—The Greatest Met of All Time
Quotes about Tom Seaver with thanks to *Baseball Almanac***:**
"Blind people come to the park just to listen to him pitch."

> —Reggie Jackson in *All Time Greatest Sports Quotes*
> (Great Quotations, Inc.)

"But Tom does everything well. He's the kind of man you'd want your kids to grow up to be like. Tom's a studious player, devoted to his profession, a loyal cat, trustworthy—everything a Boy Scout's supposed to be. In fact, we call him 'Boy Scout.'"

> —Cleon Jones

"My idea of managing is giving the ball to Tom Seaver and sitting down and watching him work."

> —Reds manager Sparky Anderson in *Late Innings*
> by Roger Angell (1982)

Seaver currently holds the Mets' career records in the following categories:

Wins: 198

ERA: 2.57

Strikeouts: 2,541

Innings Pitched: 3,045.1

Games Started: 395

Complete Games: 171

Shutouts: 44

Batters Faced: 13,191

WHIP: 1.076

Also, Home Runs Allowed (212), Bases on Balls Allowed (847), Hits Allowed (2,431), and Wild Pitches (81)

**Quiz!**

1. Which two of the following pitchers NEVER won 20 games as a Met?
   a. David Cone
   b. Tom Glavine
   c. Frank Viola
   d. Pedro Martinez

2. John Franco is first on the Mets' all-time career list for saves with 276. Which player is in second place?
   a. Armando Benitez
   b. Jesse Orosco
   c. Tug McGraw
   d. Roger McDowell

3. Who was the Mets' starting pitcher in the famous Game 6 of the 1986 World Series?

4. Who led the Mets in both victories (10) and losses (24) in the team's inaugural 1962 season?

5. As of May 2011, how many no-hitters have been thrown throughout baseball since the Mets first game in 1962?

6. Tom Seaver leads the Mets' career list for wins with 196, Dwight Gooden is second with 157, and Jerry Koosman is third with 146. Which pitcher is fourth on the Mets' all-time win list with 9l?

7. After leaving the Mets, Dwight Gooden pitched a no-hitter for which team?

8. After leaving the Mets, David Cone pitched a perfect game for which team?

9. Name the five pitchers who won at least 10 games for the pennant-winning 2000 Mets.

10. Who was the first Mets relief pitcher to make the All-Star team?

Answers

1. b. Tom Glavine and d. Pedro Martínez
2. a. Armando Benitez (160)
3. Bob Ojeda
4. Roger Craig
5. 128
6. Ron Darling
7. Yankees
8. Yankees
9. Al Leiter (13), Orel Hershiser (13), Masato Yoshii (13), Rick Reed (12), and Dennis Cook (10)
10. Tug McGraw (1972)

Footnote

If you asked most Mets fans what the greatest individual pitching performance in team history is, most would answer Tom Seaver's outing on July 9, 1969. Seaver took a perfect game into the ninth inning, when with one out Jimmy Qualls broke it up with a single. Seaver retired the next two batters and finished with a one-hitter and 11 strikeouts.

But as dominating as Seaver was that day, ultimately it was a one-hitter. Despite the fact that the Mets have never had a no-hitter, there have been 23 one-hitters in club history, the last by Aaron Heilman in '05. And while 11 strikeouts is an impressive total, the club record is 19, shared by Seaver and David Cone.

Ten

Hodges for the Hall

This is our official attempt to revive talk among members of the Hall of Fame Veterans Committee, however it's constituted at the moment, to find a place in Cooperstown for "Boys of Summer" first baseman and "Miracle Mets" manager Gil Hodges.

Hodges belongs in as one of the top sluggers of the 1950s on numerous NL pennant winners and as a premier first baseman whose powerful presence was central to the success of those great Dodgers teams.

If you're a member of the Veterans Committee and don't quite buy that, then factor in his tenure as a successful big league manager. He led a team that many thought had no business competing for the 1969 pennant to the world championship with some masterful platooning at four different positions.

For these feats as a player and as a manager, Hodges stands as one of the most beloved icons in New York sports history.

Since this book is about the Mets, let's first look at his managerial career.

Mets catcher Jerry Grote called Hodges as good a baseball man as there was around. "We enjoyed playing for him because he was always a couple of innings ahead of everyone. He knew exactly what was coming up and what was going to happen. It was great playing for him."

Donn Clendenon, the first baseman who played such an instrumental part of the Miracle Mets championship, told Marin Amoruso, the author of *Gil Hodges, The Quiet Man*, "Gil was a strong leader and he never wavered. He always believed we could win, and he made us believers too, especially the young players.

"We were a good team, no question," Clendenon continued. "We had some raw talent, we had great pitching, good defense, and we played smart heads-up baseball, but it was Gil Hodges who molded those young guys into champions."

And Grote told Amoruso, "He had an impact on everybody he touched. He got a lot of respect and he didn't have to work for it because everybody knew what kind of man he was. He was a great baseball man, and a great human being."

There were quotes similar to these from just about all the members of the '69 Mets, extolling Hodges' managerial ability, his leadership ability, and his character.

And that's before you even get to the admiration and respect he was given by all his teammates on the Dodgers in the '50s.

Roy Campanella called Hodges the "best first baseman I ever saw." And Campy joins with captain Peewee Reese to acknowledge Hodges as the true leader of the team.

All agreed that Hodges should be a lock for the Hall of Fame. And at one time it seemed that he was just that. There's nobody in baseball history who has come as close to being voted into the Hall of Fame for as many years without making it as Gil Hodges. In his 15 years on the ballot for election by the baseball writers, Hodges finished in the top five in the balloting 12 times. Everyone who received more votes than Hodges in 14 of those 15 years has been elected, and many who finished in the top 10 but behind Hodges have also gained admittance.

And what are his credentials as a player before you even add the Miracle Mets management factor?

Hodges, an ex-marine, was an eight-time All-Star and three-time Gold Glove winner. (He was well along in his career before there was a Gold Glove Award.)

He came up to the Dodgers in 1948 as a catching prospect, and there were many who believed he would have been one of the great backstops in the game.

But Roy Campanella, a Hall of Fame member since '69, was a rookie the same year, which pushed Hodges to first base and first baseman Jackie Robinson, in his second year, to second base.

And all Hodges did was develop into the best-fielding first baseman in the game and maybe one of the best of all time.

In 1960, Dodger and future Mets skipper Gil Hodges hangs out behind the batting cages before a game. *(Getty Images)*

Former Dodger teammate Carl Erskine called Hodges the best he ever saw. "He had great footwork and great range. And boy, did he have good hands. Just tremendous in size, but soft. He never dropped anything that was near him. He was so smooth he made difficult plays look easy."

He was the starting first baseman in six World Series.

Hodges was also one of the most feared sluggers in the league as part of the great Dodgers lineup with Hall of Famers Robinson, Campanella, Snider, and Reese, and former NL batting champion Carl Furillo to form a latter-day *Moiderers* Row in Brooklyn.

The Dodgers' quiet man had 11 straight seasons in which he hit 20 home runs or more, twice exceeding 40 homers in a season. He drove in 100 runs or more seven straight times. He had a slugging percentage of .500 or better nine times, and he usually walked about 75 times a year. In the decade of the '50s, Hodges was second only to teammate Snider for most home runs and RBIs in the major leagues. Between 1950 and 1959, Snider accounted for 326 home runs and 1,031 RBIs, while Hodges hit 310 dingers and drove in 1,001 runs.

Upon his retirement, Hodges held the NL record for career grand slams with 14. It has since been broken by Hank Aaron (16) and Willie McCovey (18).

In a game against the Braves in '50, Hodges became the first NL player in the 20th century to hit four home runs in a nine-inning game. And of all the Dodgers he was probably the most beloved, mostly because of the quiet strength he displayed on the field.

Hodges and Ted Kluszewski, who were considered the most powerful men in baseball at the time, were both gentle men who wouldn't hurt a soul. If there was a fight on the field, Hodges was usually the peacemaker and several times picked up the combatants and carried them away, one under each arm. He was also the most visible Dodger in the community. He married a Brooklyn girl and continued to live there with his family after his playing career ended.

Hodges was so popular that when he went into a horrendous slump, going 0–21 against the Yankees in the '52 World Series, the fans didn't boo him, they cheered him on. Many church services in Brooklyn included prayers for Hodges, and fans sent him good luck charms to help him out of the slump that continued for two months into the next season.

When the slump ended, Hodges had a great year, finishing '53 with 31 home runs and 123 RBIs and starring in the World Series.

As a player, Hodges went to L.A. when the Dodgers left and had one more shot of glory when the team won the championship over the White Sox in '59. He was taken by the Mets in the expansion draft and finished his career with New York in '62.

After managing the Washington Senators for five years, he returned to New York to take over the helm of the hapless Mets, who had never finished higher than ninth. In his second year, Hodges engineered the miracle season, and many saw his leadership as the main ingredient in the triumph.

In the book *The Greatest First Basemen of All Time,* author Donald Honig quoted Tom Seaver: "All season people kept waiting for the bubble to burst. But Gil wouldn't let it happen. He'd been through too many grueling pennant races. He never let us get too high, he wouldn't let us get too low. He instilled confidence, he made you feel like a winner, he kept you motivated."

Looking back on his years under Hodges, shortstop Bud Harrelson recalled, "Gil really made a difference in my life. He made me a better player and a better person. He was like a father to me."

Hodges died of a heart attack two days before his 48th birthday and just before the '72 baseball season began.

Eleven

The Early Mets

When the Mets opened for business in 1962, New Yorkers were excited to have National League baseball back in town.

For many fans, the success of the Yankees, with their World Series victories in 1958 and '61, had done little to soothe the pain of losing the Dodgers and Giants in '57.

But in '62 there was a new team in town. The Mets would spend their first two years at the old Polo Grounds and then move to a brand-new field, Shea Stadium in Queens, in '64.

While expectations weren't high for the team that started with the great former Yankees skipper Casey Stengel at the helm, no one could imagine how disastrous this team's performance would be on the field in that first year.

The Mets set a record for futility with a 40–120 record that stands today, finishing 10th and last in the league. And they weren't much better in '63 when they won 51 games to land at the bottom again.

It was during that first season when a frustrated Stengel asked his now-famous question: "Can't anybody here play this game?"

But, the Old Perfessor's wit and flair for the comedic helped make the team lovable despite their poor performance. So the fans flocked to the old ballpark, hoping to cheer the team to one of its rare victories and also to see some of the great NL stars such as Willie Mays, Hank Aaron, Roberto Clemente, and Frank Robinson, who hadn't visited (except to play the Yankees in the World Series) since '57.

While the victories were few and far between (as they would continue to be at the new Shea Stadium, at least until the Miracle Mets of '69), there was plenty of baseball and numerous memories created in those first two years at the Polo Grounds.

Here are a few of the highlights.

Duke Snider

In '63, in an effort to shore up their power and also to bring back memories of the Dodgers' glory days in Brooklyn, the Mets acquired the great Duke Snider.

While he was well past his prime at age 37, Snider, who had more home runs and more RBIs than any major leaguer in the decade of the 1950s, did hit his 400th career home run in his short stay with the Mets. (He would move on and finish his career with the Giants the following year.)

Snider produced only 14 home runs and 45 RBIs in 354 at-bats as a Met, but on June 14, in the first inning of a 10–3 Mets victory over the Reds at Crosley Field, The Duke cleared the fences for a historic two-run homer off Bob Purkey. Carlton Willey got the win that day, and Roger Craig finished the game with a save. The win gave Willey, who would finish the season at 9–14, a 5–5 record. And Snider wasn't the only hitting star. Outfielder Frank Thomas had four hits and four RBIs. And Ron Hunt, Tim Harkness, and Jimmy Piersall had RBI singles as well.

Jimmy Piersall

While Snider's career milestone didn't receive much attention in the New York press, Piersall, who was on the brink of hitting his 100th career home run, was determined to get a lot more publicity when he accomplished his feat.

Piersall, who was never shy about attracting public attention, had a plan to make sure that nobody would forget his 100th homer.

And on June 23 he executed his plan. Piersall popped a pitch thrown by Dallas Green of the Phillies over the short right-field fence for his 100th career homer. It would be his first and last home run as a Met.

After the ball landed in the stands, Piersall ran around the bases backward. (He went in the right direction, but he was running backward.)

"I did it good, too," Piersall said. "I even shook hands with the coach at third base."

The stunt received major coverage both in New York and in the national press, but it didn't amuse manager Casey Stengel, who was used to garnering most of the press attention at the time. He cut Piersall shortly after that, but people are still talking about the backward home run trot today.

Choo-Choo Coleman

Clarence "Choo-Choo" Coleman was a reserve catcher in those early years, and he became known for his bizarre answers to questions from the press and from Ralph Kiner on the team's postgame show, *Kiner's Korner*.

During one interview, Kiner asked Choo-Choo, "What's your wife's name and what's she like?"

Choo-Choo's answer?

"My wife's name is Mrs. Coleman and she likes me, Bub."

In another interview Kiner asked Coleman how he had gotten the name Choo-Choo. He answered, "I don't know, Ralph."

Stengel once gave Coleman, who had become one of the symbols of those awful Mets team, a left-handed compliment by saying that Choo-Choo was very fast at running to the backstop to retrieve passed balls.

Another time, the manager referred to Coleman as "the best low-ball catcher in baseball."

For his four years in the majors, the diminutive catcher had a lifetime batting average of .188.

"Marvelous Marv" Throneberry

And then there were the humorous stories about the Mets career of first baseman Marv Throneberry, who became known as "Marvelous Marv" for his frequent fielding gaffes and mental lapses.

Even though many of the stories were just part of the legend of Marvelous Marv, a few actually happened, assuring Throneberry his place in Mets history.

The most-told Throneberry incident happened on June 17, 1967, when the former Yankee tripled in a game against the Cubs. The Cubs appealed, however, and Marv was called out for failing to touch second base.

When Stengel ran out to protest the call, either the umpire or the Mets' first base coach— depending on who was telling the story— said to Casey as he ran by, "Don't bother arguing, Casey. He missed first base, too."

The next batter homered and, thanks to Throneberry's mistake, the Cubs wound up winning the game 8–7.

Again, according to legend, the Mets threw a birthday party for Stengel, and everybody received a piece of birthday cake but Throneberry. At one point, Casey supposedly went over to Marv and confided, "We was going to give you a piece, but we were afraid you'd drop it."

Throneberry became a crowd favorite, and his fame grew well beyond the reality of either his ability or ineptitude. He had a large fan club, and even after his playing days were over, he was in TV commercials capitalizing on his reputation as a screwup.

Gene Woodling

Former Yankees great Gene Woodling was nearing the end of the road when he went to the Mets during the '62 season.

Woodling hit .274 and reminisced about that season in an interview for the Society of Baseball Research's The Biography Project.

"Don't forget, I helped the Mets lose 120 games," Woodling remarked. "Casey was funny over there. He wasn't funny on the other side, with the Yankees. Bauer and I wanted to kill him. But with the Mets, I got a lot of laughs with Casey! He was probably the best public relations man that baseball ever had. He had a crowd of writers around him all the time. But Casey was a good manager, a good manager. He did win five in a row with the Yankees, and I don't think that will ever be broken."

Woodling continued talking about the Mets. "Casey just made the statement, 'None of you guys are going in (the Hall of Fame) individually, but as a team, you're a cinch!' Casey had the right idea about the Mets. He said everyone was either too young or too old."

Woodling cited Richie Ashburn, Gil Hodges, and Frank Thomas, who were nearing the end of the line but helped the team by providing some offensive punch.

"But nobody could catch the ball, and nobody could pitch! Roger Craig lost [24] games that year and probably pitched the best baseball that he pitched in his career. He looked like a traffic cop out there."

Craig Anderson

Even though everyone was too young or too old, there was one Met who looked like a genuine pitching prospect, at least for a while.

Craig Anderson was a 23-year-old right-hander who was acquired from the Cardinals in the expansion draft. He was 4–3 with St. Louis in '61, his rookie season, and showed genuine promise.

He lost his first decision for the Mets and then got his first victory in an extra-innings relief appearance on May 6. And then would come the greatest day in his major league career when he was the winning pitcher in both games of a doubleheader against the Braves on May 12.

In the first game, Anderson pitched two scoreless innings when the Mets trailed 3–2. Catcher Hobie Landrith then hit a two-run pinch-hit home run off Warren Spahn to win the game.

In the night cap, Anderson, who was the sixth Mets pitcher of the game, retired the side in the ninth inning with the score tied at 7–7. In the bottom of the ninth, Gil Hodges hit a walk-off home run and Anderson was again the winning pitcher.

But those were the last games Craig Anderson would win in his big-league career.

After a pair of saves the following week, Anderson had a 3–1 record with three saves and a 2.08 ERA. However, he went on to lose 16 straight games during that season, finishing with a 3–17 record and a 5.38 ERA.

Anderson would go 0–3 for the Mets over parts of the next two seasons for a record 19 straight losses. His 19th loss broke Roger Craig's major league record of 18, set in the team's first season.

Anderson held that record until Anthony Young went 0–27 some 30 years later.

When Young finally snapped his losing streak, Anderson sent him a message of consolation saying, "I hope you win 27 in a row."

Ed Kranepool

Kranepool was the Mets first prospect in '62, when he signed for $85,000 out of James Monroe High School in the Bronx. The 6-foot-3 left-handed-hitting first baseman may have fallen short of expectations (there was a headline when he was 19 asking, "Is Ed Kranepool Over the Hill?"), but he did develop into a solid platoon player at first base and later into one of the game's best pinch-hitters.

When his 18-year career, all with the Mets, ended, Kranepool was—and still is—the team's career leader in games (1,853), at-bats (5,436), hits (1,418), and pinch-hits (90).

When fans clamored to see the local rookie play more, manager Casey Stengel answered the fans by declaring that Kranepool "is only 17 and he runs like 30."

In '63, former Brooklyn Dodger and future Hall of Famer Duke Snider came to the Mets at the age of 36 to provide a box-office boost and to provide some left-handed power.

Snider was struggling at the bat for the Mets, but he offered to give the teenager some hitting tips and the brash young Kranepool declined, telling Snider that he wasn't doing so well himself.

Kranepool went on to play for the Mets in every season until his retirement in 1979. He was a member of the Miracle Mets World Series championship in '69 and the National League pennant winners of '73. He made the NL All-Star team in '65.

He had a career .261 average with 118 home runs and 614 RBIs. His best year was '71, when he batted .280 with a career-high 14 homers and 58 RBIs, and led the league's first basemen with a .998 fielding percentage.

Twelve

Mets Championship Teams

1969

The team that was known as the Miracle Mets won the World Series over the Baltimore Orioles in 1969, the eighth year of the New York team's existence.

In the first seven years of the franchise, the Mets lost more than 100 games five times and never finished higher than ninth in a 10-team league—and they only finished ninth twice. In their inaugural season, the Amazin' Mets set a standard for futility with 120 losses, a major league record.

But in the mid-'60s they gradually started to put a young nucleus together with homegrown prospects at first base (Ed Kranepool), shortstop (Bud Harrelson), the outfield (Cleon Jones and Ron Swoboda), and most notably pitchers (Tom Seaver and Jerry Koosman). And they sprinkled in some key players from other teams, such as catcher Jerry Grote and center fielder Tommie Agee.

In '68, Gil Hodges, a quiet forceful leader, beloved by New York fans from his days as one of the Brooklyn Dodgers' Boys of

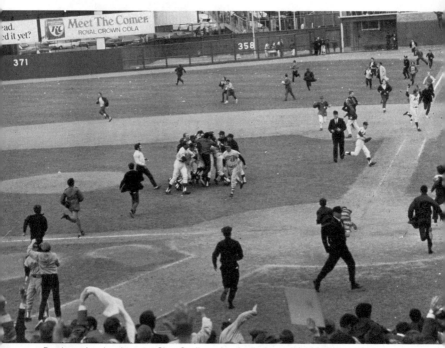

Pandemonium breaks out at Shea Stadium after the final out of the 1969 World Series.

Summer, became the manager. The first year under Hodges, the team still finished ninth, but the next year a miracle occurred.

With outstanding pitching, career years from several players, and Hodges deftly platooning players at four positions, the Miracle took place in '69. After the first 41 games that year the Mets' record was only 18–23, but then things began to change. They took off on an 11-game winning streak, the team's best ever, and they went 82–39 for the rest of the season.

When things righted themselves the Mets moved into second place, behind a star-studded Cubs team that was managed by future Hall of Famer Leo Durocher and featured three more future Cooperstown honorees in Ernie Banks, Billy Williams, and Ferguson Jenkins.

In the middle of August, the Mets were 9½ games behind the Cubs.

Then the once-lowly Mets went on one of the greatest runs in baseball history, winning 39 of their last 50 games and finishing with a 100–62 record, a full eight games ahead of the Cubs.

Tom Seaver won 25 games; Cleon Jones hit for a .340 average, third in the league; and Tommie Agee led the team with 26 home runs.

Hodges' first-base platoon of Ed Kranepool and Donn Clendenon (who was acquired during the season) combined for 23 home runs and 86 RBIs, while the right-field lefty-righty combo of Art Shamsky and Ron Swoboda delivered 23 home runs and 99 RBIs.

That was the first year of postseason division play and the Mets swept their three-game series to win the pennant and play against the heavily favored Orioles in the World Series.

After dropping the first game 4–1, the Mets, who were convinced after the loss that they could beat the Orioles, rode their surge of confidence to four straight wins, and the Miracle was complete. Clendenon, who hit three home runs in the Series, was voted as the World Series MVP.

New York Mets 1969 World Series Roster

1B: Donn Clendenon and Ed Kranepool

2B: Ken Boswell and Al Weis

SS: Bud Harrelson

3B: Wayne Garrett and Ed Charles

OF: Tommie Agee, Cleon Jones, Art Shamsky, Ron Swoboda, and Rod Gaspar

C: Jerry Grote, J.C. Martin, and Duffy Dyer

P: Tom Seaver, Jerry Koosman, Gary Gentry, Nolan Ryan, Jim McAndrew, Don Cardwell, Tug McGraw, Ron Taylor, and Cal Koonce

Quiz!

1. Who was the Baltimore Orioles pitcher in the famous shoe polish incident in the sixth inning of Game 5, when the umpire awarded Cleon Jones first base, ruling that a shoe polish smudge on the ball was evidence that the batter was hit by the pitch?

2. Which light-hitting Mets infielder tied Game 5 in the seventh inning with a solo home run?

3. Who was the Mets' winning pitcher in the fifth and deciding game?

4. In the Mets' 5–0 win in Game 3, which outfielder made game-saving catches in both the third and the seventh inning?

5. Which Mets pitcher got the save in Game 3 by pitching $2\frac{1}{3}$ innings of scoreless ball in his only appearance in the Series?

6. Which Mets pitcher threw a perfect game for six innings of Game 2 in the 2–1 win?

7. To make it to the World Series, the Mets defeated the NL Western Division champs in three games to win the first-ever League Championship Series. Which team did the Mets defeat?

8. Which Mets pitcher picked up the save in Game 2 and later went on to become a physician after he retired from baseball?

9. Which Mets outfielder, serving as a pinch-runner, scored the winning run in the 10th inning of Game 4?

10. Which Mets outfielder made a spectacular shoestring catch off the bat of Brooks Robinson that kept the Orioles from taking the lead in the top of the ninth inning?

1986

While the '69 team produced one of the most shocking world championships in baseball history, the 1986 team was expected to win because it had everything: superior starting pitching, a reliable relief force, outstanding players around the field, and as much quality depth as had ever been seen.

With young superstars Darryl Strawberry and Dwight Gooden developing, the team had fallen just short of winning the NL pennant in '84 and '85, but the pieces that were added during that time put the team in a position to take it all in '86.

Former batting champion and first baseman–supreme Keith Hernandez came over from the Cardinals in '83, and All-Star catcher and future Hall of Famer Gary Carter came in a trade with the Expos in '85. The Mets were a team with such unlimited potential that in a statement prior to the '86 season, manager Davey Johnson said, "We don't just want to win. We want to dominate."

In rolling up a record of 108–54, the Mets won the National League East by 21½ games. They went on to defeat the Astros in the NLCS in a series that ended in a 16-inning Game 6 battle that's considered one of the greatest games of all time.

In the World Series, the Mets came back from a 3–2 deficit to beat the Red Sox in historic Game 6 with a 10th-inning rally that included three clutch hits when the team was facing match point. Then there was first baseman Bill Buckner's misplay of a slow roller that went through his legs and allowed the winning run to score. The Mets would go on to win Game 7 for the second championship in franchise history.

That '86 team can certainly be listed among the strongest squads of all time.

The starting rotation, which had depth and balance, featured Bob Ojeda, who won 18; Gooden, already in his third year at age 21, who won 17; Sid Fernandez with 16 wins; and Ron Darling who won 15. Fifth starter Rick Aguilera won 10 games, and even reliever Roger McDowell won 10 games. McDowell's 22 saves and Jesse Orosco's 21 led a bullpen that gave the Mets a strong righty-lefty closer combination.

Carter led with 105 RBIs, Strawberry was the main basher with 27 home runs, and Hernandez hit .310 with an OBP of .413.

The supporting cast was led by outfielders Wilson and Lenny Dykstra, who stole 56 bases between them, and second baseman Wally Backman, who hit .320. Shortstop Rafael Santana was a light hitter but fielded his position well, and veteran third-sacker Ray Knight could both hit and field.

And behind the starters was a group of reserves that included Kevin Mitchell, Tim Teufel, Howard Johnson, and Danny Heep, who were capable of filling in for the starters with no drop-off in ability.

The Mets led the NL in batting average, runs, walks, total bases, on-base percentage, and slugging percentage. They had everything, and everyone but their fans hated that Mets team for what was perceived as their arrogance. They were a confident, hard-partying, brawling lot who took "curtain calls," coming out after home runs to acknowledge the fans.

They were hated collectively and as individuals.

"We definitely didn't take anything lightly when we stepped on the field," Strawberry told the Associated Press many years later. "We were about business when we stepped on the field. We had a swagger about ourselves."

"I think no one can deny what this team has done," said Wilson in the same article. "Regardless of the reputation that, whatever, people assume it has or whatever, it was a great team, and I think history speaks for itself."

During that season, a common refrain from outsiders sounded something like this: "I don't hate the Mets, I just hate Strawberry, Carter, Hernandez, Dykstra, Darling, and Backman. Oh, and Knight and HoJo, and Sid and Teufel and Orosco."

Gary Carter and Ray Knight celebrate after winning Game 7 of the 1986 World Series.

Some also viewed the Mets as lucky to get by both the Astros and the Red Sox, winning several unusual games. But as arrogant and lucky as this team might have been, it was certainly the greatest Mets team of all time. And it appeared headed for a long run at the top, because, aside from Carter, Wilson, Knight, and Hernandez, who were just in their early thirties, most of the team was near or approaching their peak years.

However, the dynasty was not to be. This young Mets nucleus, with the addition of David Cone, Randy Myers, and Kevin McReynolds, would make only one more run in the playoffs. In '88, they were defeated by the Dodgers in the NLCS.

Then a combination of bad personnel decisions, the lack of development by the next generation of prospects, and personal problems that beset Gooden and Strawberry made '86 the high-water mark for this generation of Mets.

But the loyal Mets fans will always have '86.

New York Mets 1986 World Series Roster

1B: Keith Hernandez

2B: Wally Backman and Tim Teufel

SS: Rafael Santana and Kevin Elster

3B: Ray Knight, Howard Johnson, and Kevin Mitchell

OF: Mookie Wilson, Lenny Dykstra, Darryl Strawberry, Danny Heep, and Lee Mazzilli

C: Gary Carter and Ed Hearn

P: Dwight Gooden, Bob Ojeda, Sid Fernandez, Ron Darling, Rick Aguilera, Roger McDowell, Randy Niemann, Doug Sisk, and Jesse Orosco

1. The Mets lost both Games 1 and 2 of the World Series. Which Mets starting pitchers took the losses in those games?

2. Who did the Mets and Red Sox defeat in the League Championship Series in order to get to the World Series?

3. Which Mets outfielder led off Game 3 with a home run?

4. Which Mets player hit a pair of home runs in Game 4 to give the New Yorkers a 6–2 win and tie the series at two games apiece?

5. Which Red Sox pitcher won his second game of the series with a 4–2 win to give the BoSox a 3–2 advantage?

6. With two out and the Mets down 5–3 in the bottom of the 10th inning of Game 6, who were the three Mets who delivered singles prior to Mookie Wilson's fateful groundball that went through Bill Buckner's legs to give the Mets a 6–5 win and even the series at three games each?

7. Who was the winning pitcher in the Mets 8–5 win in the seventh game?

8. Which Mets reliever got the saves in Games 4 and 7?

9. Carter and Dykstra each hit two homers in the Series. Name the three Mets who each smacked one homer.

10. Which member of the Mets regular-season starting rotation didn't start a game, but made three appearances in relief in the World Series?

Answers

1. Dwight Gooden in Game 1 and Ron Darling in Game 2

2. The Red Sox defeated the California Angels and the Mets defeated the Houston Astros.

3. Lenny Dykstra

4. Gary Carter

5. Bruce Hurst

6. Gary Carter, Kevin Mitchell, and Ray Knight

7. Roger McDowell

8. Jesse Orosco

9. Tim Teufel in Game 5, Ray Knight and Darryl Strawberry in Game 7

10. Sid Fernandez

Thirteen

The Superstar Quiz

Gooden delivers a pitch to the Cardinals during his historic 1985 season.

Quiz!

Dwight Gooden

1. Dwight Gooden won the NL Cy Young Award in 1985. Who won the AL Cy Young that year?
2. Who was the NL Cy Young Award winner in 1984?
3. Who was the NL Cy Young Award winner in 1986?
4. What was Gooden's cheering section at Shea Stadium called?
5. In 1984, Gooden won 17 games as a rookie. Who holds the Mets record for games won by a rookie pitcher, and in what year did he do it?
6. How many times did Gooden strike out at least 200 batters in a season?
7. How many World Series champions did Gooden play for?
8. Gooden pitched a no-hitter for the Yankees in 1996 with a win over which team?
9. Who caught Gooden's no-hitter?
10. Dwight Gooden played for three of these four teams during his major league career. Which team did he *not* play for?
    a. Devil Rays
    b. Cardinals
    c. Astros
    d. Indians

Answers

1. Bret Saberhagen, Royals
2. Rick Sutcliffe, Cubs
3. Mike Scott, Astros
4. The K Corner
5. Jerry Koosman won 19 games in 1968.
6. Four times
7. Three: Mets once (1986) and Yankees twice (1996 and 2000)
8. Seattle Mariners
9. Joe Girardi
10. b. Cardinals

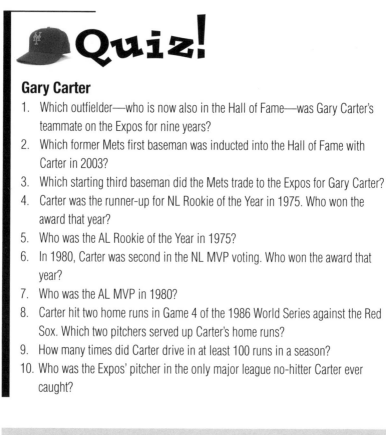

Gary Carter

1. Which outfielder—who is now also in the Hall of Fame—was Gary Carter's teammate on the Expos for nine years?

2. Which former Mets first baseman was inducted into the Hall of Fame with Carter in 2003?

3. Which starting third baseman did the Mets trade to the Expos for Gary Carter?

4. Carter was the runner-up for NL Rookie of the Year in 1975. Who won the award that year?

5. Who was the AL Rookie of the Year in 1975?

6. In 1980, Carter was second in the NL MVP voting. Who won the award that year?

7. Who was the AL MVP in 1980?

8. Carter hit two home runs in Game 4 of the 1986 World Series against the Red Sox. Which two pitchers served up Carter's home runs?

9. How many times did Carter drive in at least 100 runs in a season?

10. Who was the Expos' pitcher in the only major league no-hitter Carter ever caught?

Answers

1. Andre Dawson
2. Eddie Murray
3. Hubie Brooks
4. John Montefusco
5. Fred Lynn
6. Mike Schmidt
7. George Brett
8. Al Nipper and Steve Crawford
9. Four times: twice with the Expos (101 in 1980 and 106 in 1984) and twice with the Mets (100 in 1985 and 106 in 1986).
10. Charlie Lea in 1981

Tom Seaver

1. What four players did the Mets receive when they traded Tom Seaver to the Reds in 1977?

2. Tom is Seaver's middle name. What is his first name?

3. In 1966, before signing with the Mets, Seaver signed a contract with another NL team, but the contract was voided on a technicality. What was the team?

4. What team was Tom Seaver pitching for when he threw his 300th career victory?

5. Who was Seaver's catcher when he pitched his 300th win?

6. In what ballpark did Seaver pitch his 300th win?

7. Seaver won the NL Cy Young Award in 1969, 1973, and 1975. Who won the AL Cy Young in each of those three seasons?

8. Tom Seaver pitched one no-hitter in his career. Which team was Seaver pitching for when he tossed his no-hitter?

9. Against which team did Seaver pitch his no-hitter?

10. Seaver is No. 1 on the Mets' all-time list in wins, ERA, and strikeouts. Name the pitcher(s) who ranks second for the Mets in each of those categories.

Willie Mays

1. Which modern baseball great is Willie Mays' godson?
2. Which Giants pitcher threw the pitch in the 1954 World Series that the Indians' Vic Wertz hit to deep center, where Mays made "The Catch"?
3. Who was Willie's first manager with the Giants?
4. How many times did Mays finish in the top 10 in NL MVP voting?
5. Did Mays ever win the MVP? And if so, how many times and in what years?
6. Willie was the NL Rookie of the Year in 1951. Who won the award in the AL that year?
7. How many times was Willie the NL stolen-base champion and in what year or years?
8. As a member of the Mets, Willie hit his 660th and final home run in 1973. Against which Reds pitcher did he hit it?
9. Which Hall of Famer and Negro League great was Willie's roommate in his last year in the minors with the Minneapolis Millers?
10. Who are the seven pitchers who were 20-game winners when they were Willie's teammates with the Giants from 1951 to 1972?

Answers

1. Barry Bonds
2. Don Liddle
3. Leo Durocher
4. 12 times
5. He was the MVP in 1954 and 1965.
6. Gil McDougald, Yankees
7. Four times in a row, 1956 to 1959
8. Don Gullett
9. Ray Dandridge
10. Sal Maglie, Larry Jansen, Johnny Antonelli, Juan Marichal, Gaylord Perry, and Mike McCormick (Tom Seaver also won 20 games with the Mets when he was Willie's teammate).

Mike Piazza

1. Mike Piazza owns the major league record for most career home runs by a catcher (427) and also most home runs by a catcher while playing as a catcher (396). As of 2011, who's second in each category?

2. Piazza is currently fourth on the Mets' all-time list of highest batting average as a Met with a .296 average. Who are the three men ahead of him?

3. Piazza won the NL Rookie of the Year Award for 1993. Who was the AL winner?

4. Piazza is third on the Mets' all-time RBI list with 655. Who are the two men ahead of him?

5. Piazza is second on the Mets' all-time home run list with 220. Who is first on the list and who is third?

6. Piazza finished second in the NL MVP voting in both 1996 and 1997. Who were the winners?

7. How many times was Piazza selected for the All-Star Game?

8. Who are the only two players besides Piazza to hit a World Series home run in both Yankee Stadium and Shea Stadium?

9. Piazza is one of nine catchers to have won a major league Rookie of the Year Award. Name five of the other eight.

10. How many times did Piazza win the Silver Slugger Award?

Keith Hernandez

1. In 1979, Keith Hernandez was the co-winner of the NL MVP award. It was the only time two people received exactly the same number of votes. With whom did Keith share the award?

2. Who was the AL MVP that year?

3. Which Hall of Fame pitcher did Hernandez—then a Cardinal—homer against in Game 6 of the 1982 World Series?

4. In 1985, Hernandez, as a Met, finished eighth in the NL MVP voting. Two of his teammates were among the seven players who finished ahead of him. Who were they?

5. In 1986, Carter and Hernandez finished third and fourth in the NL MVP Award voting. Who was the MVP that year?

6. Identify the batting statistic that was only kept officially from 1980 to 1988 in which Hernandez is the major league career leader.

7. How many Gold Gloves did Hernandez win in his career?

8. In how many of his full seasons in the majors did Hernandez hit .300 or better?
9. What Number did Keith Hernandez wear when he was a member of the Mets?
10. Which of Hernandez's teammates was supposedly "the second spitter" who spat on the characters Kramer and Newman on an episode of *Seinfeld*?

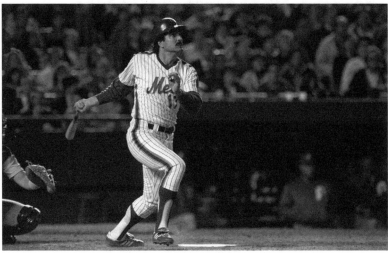

Keith Hernandez puts one over the right-field fence at Shea.

Fourteen

Mets Match Game

These 10 former Mets are more identified with another major league team. Match the player with his primary team.

1. Duke Snider
2. Warren Spahn
3. Willie Mays
4. Ken Boyer
5. Yogi Berra
6. Richie Ashburn
7. George Foster
8. Bob Friend
9. Gary Carter
10. Carlos Delgado

A. Reds
B. Blue Jays
C. Dodgers
D. Pirates
E. Cardinals
F. Expos
G. Braves
H. Yankees
I. Giants
J. Phillies

Answers
1.C 2.G 3.I 4.E 5.H 6.J 7.A 8.D 9.F 10.B

Match the Mets player with his nickname

1.	Clarence Coleman	A. Pumpsie
2.	Gary Carter	B. Turk
3.	Dick Stuart	C. Roadblock
4.	Elijah Green	D. Mookie
5.	Frank McGraw	E. Vinegar Bend
6.	Steven Wendell	F. Choo-Choo
7.	Don Zimmer	G. Tug
8.	Sherman Jones	H. Popeye
9.	William Wilson	I. Kid
10.	Wilmer Mizell	J. Dr. Strangeglove

Answers
1.F 2.I 3.J 4.A 5.G 6.B 7.H 8.C 9.D 10.E

Match the Mets player with his brother who also played in the major leagues

1.	Tom Glavine	A. Larry
2.	Ken Boyer	B. Ramon
3.	Bob Aspromonte	C. Greg
4.	Mike Maddux	D. Mike
5.	Jesus Alou	E. Frank
6.	Norm Sherry	F. Livan
7.	Marv Throneberry	G. Clete
8.	Joe Torre	H. Mateo
9.	Orlando Hernandez	I. Faye
10.	Pedro Martinez	K. Ken

Answers
1.D 2.G 3.K 4.C 5.H 6.A 7.I 8.E 9.F 10.B

Match the Mets player with his father who also played in the major leagues

1.	Todd Hundley	A.	Hal
2.	Scott Hairston	B.	Camilo
3.	Brian McRae	C.	Al
4.	Del Unser	D.	Bob
5.	Ike Davis	E.	Felipe
6.	Darren Oliver	F.	Floyd
7.	Roberto Alomar	G.	Jerry
8.	Brian Bannister	H.	Ron
9.	Moises Alou	I.	Randy
10.	Mark Carreon	J.	Sandy

Answers
1.I 2.G 3.A 4.C 5.H 6.D 7.J 8.F 9.E 10.B

Fifteen

Honors

Retired Numbers

42: Jackie Robinson, Retired throughout baseball in 1997
41: Tom Seaver, 1988, Only Mets player to have his number retired
37: Casey Stengel, 1965, Manager
14: Gil Hodges, 1973, Manager

New York Mets in the Baseball Hall of Fame

Year Inducted — Year(s) as a Mets Player

Yogi Berra, 1972 — 1965
Warren Spahn, 1973 — 1965
Willie Mays, 1979 — 1963
Duke Snider, 1980 — 1963
Tom Seaver, 1992 — 1967-77, 1987
Richie Ashburn, 1995 — 1962
Nolan Ryan, 1991 — 1966-1971
Gary Carter, 2003 — 1985-89
Eddie Murray, 2003 — 1992-93
Rickey Henderson, 2009 — 1999-2000
Roberto Alomar, 2011 — 2002-03
Casey Stengel (Manager), 1966 — 1962-65

New York Mets Who Should Be in the Baseball Hall of Fame
Ken Boyer
Keith Hernandez
Gil Hodges
Joe Torre

The New York Mets Hall of Fame
1981, Joan Payson and Casey Stengel
1982, Gil Hodges, George Weiss, and Bud Harrelson
1983, Johnny Murphy and Bill Shea
1984, Ralph Kiner, Bob Murphy, and Lindsey Nelson
1986, Rusty Staub
1988, Tom Seaver
1989, Jerry Koosman
1990, Ed Kranepool
1991, Cleon Jones
1992, Jerry Grote
1993, Tug McGraw
1996, Mookie Wilson
1997, Keith Hernandez
2001, Gary Carter
2002, Tommie Agee
2010, Frank Cashen, Dwight Gooden, Davey Johnson, and Darryl
    Strawberry

Mets Multiple All-Stars
First Base: Keith Hernandez (3)
Second Base: Ron Hunt (2)
Shortstop: Bud Harrelson (2) and Jose Reyes (3)
Third Base: Howard Johnson (2) and David Wright (5)
Outfield: Carlos Beltran (5), Bobby Bonilla (2), Willie Mays (2), and
    Darryl Strawberry (7)

Catcher: Gary Carter (4), Jerry Grote (2), Todd Hundley (2), Mike
     Piazza (7), and John Stearns (4)
Pitcher: David Cone (2), Sid Fernandez (2), Tom Glavine (2), Dwight
     Gooden (4), Jerry Koosman (2), Pedro Martinez (2), Jon Matlack
     (3), Jesse Orosco (2), Rick Reed (2), Tom Seaver (9), Frank Viola
     (2), and Billy Wagner (2)

Awards and Leaders

National League Rookie of the Year
Tom Seaver, 1967
Jon Matlack, 1972
Darryl Strawberry, 1983
Dwight Gooden, 1984

World Series MVP
Donn Clendenon, 1969
Ray Knight, 1986

All-Star Game MVP
Jon Matlack, 1975 (co-MVP with Bill Madlock)

Comeback Player of the Year
Ray Knight, 1986
Rickey Henderson, 1999
Fernando Tatis, 2008

Roberto Clemente Award
Gary Carter, 1989
Al Leiter, 2001
Carlos Delgado, 2006

Home Run Champions
Dave Kingman, (48) 1979
Darryl Strawberry, (39) 1988

RBI Champion
Howard Johnson, (117) 1991

Runs Champion
Howard Johnson, (104, tied with Will Clark and Ryne Sandburg) 1989

Stolen Base Champion
Jose Reyes, 2005 (60), 2006 (64), and 2007 (78)

Silver Slugger Awards
First Base: Keith Hernandez, 1984
Second Base: Edgardo Alfonzo, 1999
Shortstop: Joes Reyes, 2006
Third Base: Howard Johnson, 1989 and 1991, and David Wright 2007 and 2008
Outfield: Daryl Strawberry, 1988 and 1990, and Carlos Beltran, 2006 and 2007
Catcher: Gary Carter, 1985 and 1986, and Mike Piazza 1998, 1999, 2000, 2001, and 2002
Pitcher: Dwight Gooden, 1992, and Mike Hampton, 2006 and 2007

Gold Gloves
First Base: Keith Hernandez, 1983, 1984, 1985, 1986, 1987, and 1988
Second Base: Doug Flynn, 1980
Shortstop: Bud Harrelson, 1973, and Rey Ordonez, 1997, 1998, and 1999

Third Base: Robin Ventura, 1999, and David Wright, 2007 and 2008
Outfield: Tommie Agee, 1970, and Carlos Beltran, 2006, 2007, and 2008
Pitcher: Ron Darling, 1989

Cy Young Award
Tom Seaver, 1969, 1973, and 1975
Dwight Gooden, 1985

Pitching Triple Crown
Dwight Gooden, 1985: ERA, 1.53; Wins, 24; Strikeouts, 268

Strikeout Champions
Tom Seaver, 1970 (283), 1971 (289), 1973 (251), 1975 (243), and 1976 (235)
Dwight Gooden, 1984 (276) and 1985 (268)
David Cone, 1990 (233) and 1991 (241)

ERA Champions
Tom Seaver, 1970 (2.82), 1971 (1.76), and 1973 (2.01)
Craig Swan, 1978 (2.43)
Dwight Gooden, 1985 (1.53)
Johan Santana, 2008 (2.53)

Relief Man of the Year
John Franco, 1990 and 1994
Armando Benitez, 2001

Sixteen

All-Time Mets Teams

Players from the New York Metropolitan Area All-Stars

You've got some career Mets such as Kranepool and Franco; some who gave us significant time like Mazzilli, Lynch, and Bonilla; and most of the others who just stopped by their home town for a cup of coffee. We just ask that New Yorkers welcome Cerone, Maddox, and DiPoto who are from...New Jersey.

The team is solid around the field and pretty good at the top of the rotation with Candelaris, Viola, and Shaw, but we're in need of pitching depth. Torre, Singleton, and Bonilla supply the power and Davis is a two-time NL batting champ.

First Base: Ed Kranepool and Mike Jorgensen
Second Base: Willie Randolph and Damion Easley
Shortstop: Shawon Dunston and John Valentin
Third Base: Joe Torre, Joe Foy, and Bob Aspromonte
Outfield: Lee Mazzilli, Tommy Davis, Bobby Bonilla, Ken Singleton, John Cangelosi, and Elliott Maddox (NJ)
Catcher: Paul Lo Duca and Rick Cerone (NJ)
Pitcher: John Candelaria, Larry Bearnarth, Pete Falcone, John Franco, Ed Lynch, Joe Sambito, Bob Shaw, Frank Viola, and Jerry DiPoto (NJ)

New York Mets Managers All-Stars

With all due respect to Green and Bamberger, pitching is a big hole on this team. We suggest for the future that the Mets hire some pitchers to manage the club. Other than that, we're strong all the way around. Outfield depth is suspect, but an outfield of Howard, Valentine, and Stengel isn't bad. You can also use Yogi, who played there late in his career. Torre gives the team flexibility.

First Base: Gil Hodges

Second Base: Willie Randolph, Davey Johnson, and Jerry Manuel

Shortstop: Bud Harrelson, Roy McMillan, Salty Parker, and Terry Collins

Third Base: Joe Torre, Mike Cubbage, and Art Howe

Outfield: Frank Howard, Bobby Valentine, Casey Stengel, and Joe Frazier

Catcher: Yogi Berra, Wes Westrum, and Jeff Torborg

Pitcher: Dallas Green and George Bamberger

The All-Time Mets All-Stars

This is not just a starting lineup, it's a list of outstanding players who played at one time for the Mets. While some gave the Mets their best years, many were big stars for other teams who came to the Mets for one more stab at glory or to finish their careers.

Wow, would the Mets have had a glorious history if they could have had all of these players during their best years. Think what a rotation of Seaver, Spahn, Ryan, Martinez, and Gooden could do against any team you could put together at any time in baseball history.

The same is true of the fielders. There's at least one Hall of Famer, possible future Hall of Famer (Reyes?), or should-be Hall of Famer at every position. Shortstop is a little thin on the hitting.

Reyes and Fregosi are good, but McMillan and Harrelson give you everything you need on defense.

There's actually two or three teams worth of talent here. But who starts? That's the question. I've put my choices in bold.

First Base: **Eddie Murray**, Carlos Delgado, Gil Hodges, Keith Hernandez, and Mo Vaughn

Second Base: **Roberto Alomar**, Willie Randolph, and Edgardo Alfonzo

Shortstop: **Jose Reyes,** Roy McMillan, Bud Harrelson, and Jim Fregosi

Third Base: Ken Boyer, **David Wright**, Robin Ventura, and **Joe Torre (DH, C)**

Outfield: **Willie Mays, Rickey Henderson, Duke Snider, Darryl Strawberry (DH),** Tommy Davis, Rusty Staub, Richie Ashburn, Cleon Jones, Lenny Dykstra, Mookie Wilson, Gus Bell, Carlos Beltran, Jim Piersall, Frank Thomas, Gene Woodling, Gary Sheffield, Amos Otis, Ken Singleton, George Foster, Shawn Green, and Cliff Floyd

Catcher: Gary Carter, Mike Piazza, **Yogi Berra,** Jerry Grote, and John Stearns

Pitcher: **Tom Seaver, Warren Spahn , Nolan Ryan, Pedro Martinez, Dwight Gooden**, Jerry Koosman, David Cone, Tom Glavine, Johann Santana, John Franco, Armando Benitez, Jesse Orosco, Tug McGraw, Mickey Lolich, Randy Meyers, Francisco Rodriguez, Ron Darling, Frank Viola, Orel Hershiser, Bob Friend, Al Leiter, Frank Lary, Clem Labine, Mike Marshall, Billy Wagner, Rick Aguilera, Bob Ojeda, Sid Fernandez, Roger McDowell, and Jeff Reardon

All-Cool-Name Team

This team isn't as great as the ones that can be put together for those franchises whose history goes back to the early 19th century, but there are some gems nevertheless. We're relying on nicknames to fill out the lineup. And you'll notice that we don't really have a shortstop. Wilbur Huckle never played in the majors, but he was a prospect for several years and fans of the early Mets knew about him and eagerly awaited his arrival in New York, which never came. Wilbur, welcome to the big leagues. To be honest, I have no recollection of Esix Snead, but he sounds like a Dickens character, so he's okay by me. Maybe Huckle and Snead can room together on the road.

Hershiser is the ace, of course, and he'll probably have to pitch on two days' rest for us to have a chance in any pretend league we're in. Whatever offense we have will have to come from Darryl and Mookie. (This will be a selling ballclub by May 1.)

First Base: Kelvin Torve and Rico Brogna

Second Base: Tim Teufel

Shortstop: Wilbur Huckle (a prospect makes the team even though he never appeared in a major league game)

Third Base: Pumpsie Green and Butch Huskey

Outfield: Lastings Milledge, Darryl Strawberry, Mookie Wilson, Esix Snead, Benny Agbayani, Amos Otis, and Xavier Nady

Catcher: Mackey Sasser and Choo-Choo Coleman

Pitcher: Mauro Gozzo, Ambiorix Burgos, Jae Seo, Mac Scarce, Vinegar Bend Mizell, Roadblock Jones, and Orel Hershiser

Seventeen

Kiner and Stengel Speak

Ralph Kiner, a Mets broadcaster since the team began in 1962, became famous for his humorous quotes and his malaprops.

As of 2011, Kiner is second only to the Dodgers' Vin Scully in length of service among major league announcers. He's also hosted the Mets' postgame show *Kiner's Korner* for many years. Of course, Kiner's Korner was the name given to the place in left field at Forbes Field in Pittsburgh to where the right-handed-hitting slugger planted his home runs when he was a member of the Pirates.

On the way to being named to the Hall of Fame, Kiner was a six-time All-Star who led the league in home runs in his first seven years in the majors, including a career-high 54 homers in 1949.

Kiner, who was one of the first big leaguers to earn $100,000, played for woeful Pirates teams that usually finished in the cellar. So, when he went to ask for a salary increase in 1952, general manager Branch Rickey told him, "We finished last with you, and we can finish last without you."

Rickey traded Kiner to the Cubs in '53, and the slugger finished his career in '55 as a member of the Indians because of an injured back.

He was elected to the Hall of Fame by the baseball writers in his last year on the ballot in 1975.

"Kiner-isms"

"Singles hitters drive Fords, home run hitters drive Cadillacs."

"Hello everybody. Welcome to *Kiner's Corner*. This is...uh...I'm... uh..."

"If Casey Stengel were alive today, he'd be spinning in his grave."

"The Hall of Fame ceremonies are on the 31st and 32nd of July."

"On Father's Day, we again wish you all happy birthday."

"Two-thirds of the earth is covered by water. The other third is covered by Garry Maddox." (Actually, a great ad lib about the Phillies' outstanding center fielder)

"The Mets have gotten their leadoff batter on only once this inning."

"You know what they say about Chicago. If you don't like the weather, wait fifteen minutes."

"Solo homers usually come with no one on base."

"This one deep to right, and it is way back, going, going, it is gone, no, it's off of the top of the wall."

"There's a lot of heredity in that family."

"It's [Phil Niekro's knuckleball] like watching Mario Andretti park a car."

"Tony Gwynn was named player of the year for April."

"Kevin McReynolds stops at third and he scores."

(As Gary Carter came to the plate.) "Now up to bat for the Mets is Gary Cooper."

"All of the Mets' road wins against the Dodgers this year occurred at Dodger Stadium."

"Jose DeLeon, in his career, has 73 wins and 105 RBIs."

"Don Sutton lost 13 games in a row without winning a ballgame."

"The reason the Mets have played so well at Shea this year is they have the best home record in baseball."

"Darryl Strawberry has been voted to the Hall of Fame five years in a row."

"Bruce Sutter's going to be out of action the rest of his career."

"Cadillacs are down at the end of the bat."

"All of his saves have come in relief appearances."

Manager Casey Stengel was famous for decades during his playing and Hall of Fame managerial career as an imp and a character with many stories attesting to his wit and clownishness. As a manager, he entertained writers, fellow baseball people, and the public with his wry observations and his new language, "Stengelese," a long, meandering method of answering questions and telling stories that bordered on double-talk. But according to those who knew him, he "always had a point." While he was famous for Stengelese, he didn't get as much attention for his playful and sometimes caustic wit when he managed the great Yankees teams as he would later when he managed the hapless Mets and would use his brand of humor as a distraction to grab attention away from the ineptitude on the field. Here are some of Casey's greatest quotes about his years with the Mets.

"Stengelese"

"Can't anybody here play this game?"

"We've got to learn how to stay out of triple plays."

"I've been in the game 100 years, but the Mets have shown me more ways to lose than I ever knew existed."

"The only thing worse than a Mets game is a Mets doubleheader."

"President Johnson wanted to see poverty, so he came to see my team."

"Our first Mets game was April 10, 1962. And it was our best game. It was rained out."

"You have to have a catcher, because if you don't you're likely to have a lot of passed balls."

Casey was asked if the altitude contributed to the Mets loss of an exhibition game in Mexico City. "Not a bit; we lose at any altitude."

"Chris Cannizzaro is the only defensive catcher who can't catch."

"The Mets are a much improved ballclub, now we lose in extra innings!"

When asked how it felt to be 75 years old, Casey replied, "Most people my age are dead at the present time."

On rookie first baseman Ed Kranepool: "He's only 17 and he runs like he's 30."

"It's wonderful to meet so many friends that I didn't used to like."

"He's only 20 years old and with a good chance in 10 years of being 30." On one of his Mets prospects.

"Don't cut my throat. I may want to do that later, myself."

Of catcher Chris Cannizzaro, Casey said, "He calls for the curve ball so much. He can't hit it, so he figures nobody else can."

And about pitcher Jay Hook who had a genius IQ: "You should forget about those big words. You can't get 'em out in the library."

About infielder Don Zimmer when he got two hits to break out of an 0-for-34 slump: "We gotta trade him while he's still hot."

About outfielder Ron Swoboda: "He has amazing strength, amazing power. He can grind the dust out of the bat. He will be great, super, even wonderful. Now, if he can only learn to catch a fly ball."

"Gil Hodges fields better on one leg than anybody else I got on two."

Casey Stengel was particularly impressed by Shea Stadium. "With these escalators you won't get a heart attack going to your seats. Anybody can come out and see us, women, men, and children, because we got 50 bathrooms all over the place."

"I got players with bad watches—they can't tell midnight from noon."

After a Met hit a homer over the short right-field porch at the Polo Grounds: "Ain't that something! Just when my fellers learn to hit the ball in this park, they're gonna tear the thing down."—From *Baseball Forever*, by Ralph Kiner with Danny Peary

About the 1969 Mets: "This club plays better baseball now. Some of them look fairly alert."

"Without losers, where would the winners be?"

The inimitable Casey Stengel at his clubhouse desk in 1963